Grc

"At last! The small group world has finally been given rock solid research that proves what it takes to create groups that are gospel-centered, relationally bonded, evangelistically effective, disciple-making, and that multiply for Kingdom purposes. If you're a senior pastor, groups pastor, group member, education minister, or a Sunday School teacher, I'm begging you to read this book--then do what it says to do. Read this book first! There is a plethora of fantastic books written by some of the best thinkers in the groups world. Read as many of them as you can. But, READ THIS BOOK FIRST! *Groups That Thrive* unearths indisputable research that will guide you to practices that create groups that really do evangelize and make disciples. The vision God has given me is to see, 'A biblical small group within walking distance of every person on the planet making disciples that make disciples.' *Groups That Thrive* reveals the rock- solid research and the practices necessary to see this vision become a reality."

> —Rick Howerton, author, Small Group enthusiast, and Church Consultant with Kentucky Baptist Convention

"Every church leader wants to promote healthy small groups. Many have personal opinions about what produces healthy small groups. The challenge is actually knowing what makes small groups healthy. This is why *Groups That Thrive: 8 Surprising Discoveries About Life-giving Small Groups* is so valuable. It goes beyond opinions and hunches. Joel Comiskey and Jim Egli instead use research driven findings to define and describe the real elements of healthy small groups. It's a must read for anyone involved in small group ministry."

> —Steve Gladen, Saddleback Church, Pastor of Small Groups, author of book, *Planning Small Groups With Purpose*

"Most of us who lead vibrant, healthy small groups probably don't know why they are so vibrant and healthy. Jim and Joel unpack those key contributing elements through their vast research. As more group leaders and pastors implement these key findings God will bless the effort with strong groups. We need more research based books like this in the small groups discipline!"

> —Pastor Bill Search, author of *The Essential Guide for Small Group Leaders* and *Simple Small Groups*

"This book embodies everything I believe and practice about leading small groups successfully! 23 years ago I was taught to do these exact things and I've spent the last 23 years doing them and teaching group leaders under my ministry to do them as well. Joel and Jim's book isn't some starry-eyed theory about how small groups are supposed to work, but proven and tried ways of doing small groups well. Ingest this book and start doing every practice it suggests. Put it in the hands of every small group leader you know. Do things this way and your groups will thrive!"

> —Jay Firebaugh, Director of Small Groups, New Life Church, Gahanna/ Columbus, OH

"I love the emphasis on thriving groups. Often in small-group ministry, we're stuck in reactionary mode—we're reacting and responding to issues that arise. But Comiskey prompts us to consider how we can proactively set up small groups to thrive and be all they're meant to be, all based on research. This leads to healthy relationships, abundant spiritual growth, and a deep connection to the mission of God."
        —Amy Jackson, Associate Publisher for SmallGroups.com

"Reading *Groups that Thrive* is a significant step in my small group journey. With powerful new analytics, this book continues the process of refining and balancing my view of groups ministry. This is a must-read for any groups practitioner, leader and pastor!"
        —Andrew Mason, Founder, SmallGroupChurches.com

Groups that Thrive

Groups that Thrive

8 Surprising Discoveries about
Life-Giving Small Groups

**Joel Comiskey
with Jim Egli**

Copyright ©2018 by Joel Comiskey with Jim Egli

Published by CCS Publishing
23890 Brittlebush Circle
Moreno Valley, CA 92557 USA
1-888-511-9995

Printed in the United States of America.

Cover design: Jason Klanderud
Editor: Scott Boren

ISBN: 9781935789901
LCCN: 2017937626

CCS Publishing is the book-publishing division of Joel Comiskey Group, a resource and coaching ministry dedicated to equipping leaders for cell-based ministry. Find us on the World Wide Web at www.joelcomiskeygroup.com

TABLE OF CONTENTS

DEDICATION

To Celyce Comiskey (Joel's best friend and marriage/ministry partner for 30-years) and Vicki Egli (Jim's amazing partner in life and ministry for the last 40 years)

ACKNOWLEDGEMENTS

The hidden figure of this study is Wei Wang, a researcher at Northwestern University in Evanston, Illinois. He performed the statistical analysis of the data that resulted from surveys completed by thousands of small group leaders. The analysis of this data serves as the basis for the surprising insights of this book. Without his help, this book would not have been possible.

Eric Glover served as a volunteer copy editor and spent a lot of time pouring over the grammatical details of this book. He offered detailed corrections on punctuation and sentence structure. Jim and I really appreciated his effort.

Brian McClemore's gave us a rigorous edit of the final draft. He offered detail advice on sentence structure, meaning, and challenged many generalizations. We listened to his advice and changed many sentences as a result of his excellent effort.

Rae Sholt Rae gave us insightful observations and critical corrections. He noticed empty footnotes and incorrect Scripture passages, while suggesting additional Scripture. He helped clarify terms and unclear sentences. Jim and I are very thankful for his volunteer effort in perfecting this book.

Jay Stanwood once again helped simplify unclear statements while providing better alternatives. He provided a thorough grammatical edit of the text, and this current book is much better because of his edit.

Melissa Egli looked at an early draft of the book and gave broad, general insight. We really appreciated her positive feedback at a time when the draft was very rough. Her edit gave needful perspective and confidence to press ahead.

Sue Standifer graciously looked at the final version and used her skills in copy-editing to weed out errors and offer valuable advice. We are thankful for her help.

Scott Boren, our primary editor, guided us to understand the big picture and how to organize the material. He took a very rough draft, bogged down in quotes and unnecessary details, and helped us navigate our way to the final draft. His expertise guided us throughout the process, and we're very grateful for his editing.

INTRODUCTION

In 1990, my wife and I moved to South America to serve as missionaries to Ecuador. As a part of our preparation, we lived in Costa Rica for one year to learn the Spanish language. A new Costa Rican friend, Martin, invited me to explore one of the vast Costa Rican rain forests. We hopped on a long-distance bus, rode miles into the dense rain forest, passed through a long tunnel, and then Martin asked the driver to let us off. We then began to climb over the tunnel to the other side.

what causes groups to thrive?

I felt overwhelmed as I was surrounded by giant trees, plants, grasses, and the virgin mountainside. It was a world of lush vegetation, streams, and insects. We even had to flee a hive of angry hornets while sliding down a waterfall. Finally, we made it to the other side, wet, dirty, and exhausted.

This experience opened my eyes to life that thrives. This pristine and secluded rain forest is a wild, wet, and perfect environment for green life to thrive. This book is about thriving and flourishing. It's about creating an environment where life has a chance to spread and organically and naturally extend itself in every direction. Just like green foliage needs the right mixture of sun, soil, and water, thriving groups require a healthy atmosphere. Sadly, many small groups today do not thrive. They limp along year after year and eventually close, stopping short of the life that God has for them.

Just like that Costa Rican rain forest, groups that thrive don't happen by chance nor simply because people want their groups to flourish. Thriving communities require a supernatural mix of prayer and Spirit-led anointing that makes a way for everyone to participate, for the healing presence of God, and for vibrant life that blesses others. This book explores how your group can thrive.

> *Life-giving groups begin by imagining the kind of group that you want.*

Living the Dream in a Thriving Group

Imagine that you are a part of a thriving small group. What we imagine or dream about regarding the kind of group we hope for will shape the way we form our groups. If you want to create a life-giving garden, it begins by imagining the kind of garden that you want.

In a thriving group, people feel loved, accepted, and embraced. No one hides behind religious platitudes or feels

> *The meeting is like a gathering of good friends with the presence of Jesus in their midst.*

the need to perform in order to measure up. Group members laugh, cry, and listen deeply to each other.

The leader does not force his or her way or control the group meetings in order to try to make the group thrive. Instead, he or she creates a safe place for everyone to share. Instead of long monologues of Bible study facts, the effective leader is a facilitator who asks questions so that everyone can get involved. Even more, there is time and freedom for people to use their spiritual gifts so that people can be encouraged and built up as Paul said in 1 Corinthians 14.

The meeting is like a gathering of good friends with the presence of Jesus in their midst. Sometimes there are difficult conversations, but the group members are committed to working through any issue.

I pray that your group is experiencing this vision. Where it falls short, know that God can bring forth life. Your group need not continue as it is now. New paths can be charted that will bring new life and new hope.

In Search of Paths of Thriving

The task of describing a thriving small group motivated Jim Egli and me to study the difference between a so-so, run-of-the-mill meeting and a life-giving group that is more than a religious meeting. We surveyed 1,800 small group members and leaders from around the world. This data was added to Jim's previous investigation of over 3,000 small group leaders. The details of the research design and data are included in the appendix for those who are interested in such matters.

Even though Jim and I together have been working with small groups for over five decades, we were surprised by what we found. Some of the conclusions seemed to go against logic and challenge common understanding about what makes a group work well. We simply followed the evidence and now share what we discovered.

> *The best way to multiply a group is to develop each member's potential.*

Most books on small groups are written for group leaders or pastors. While this book has much to say to leaders, we also want it to encourage group members. After all, each member is a potential facilitator, and, in fact, the best groups allow each person to lead parts of the group meetings. Someone does need to take responsibility, but the best leaders are team players and see each member as an active participant and potential facilitator. The best way to multiply a group is to develop each member's potential.

Surprising Paths

As a kid growing up in Long Beach, California, I loved Fridays. When I came home from Emerson Elementary School, I knew my mom would surprise me by hiding a candy bar, Twinkie, or another treat under my pillow. This book is about surprises.

They are surprising discoveries that go against common assumptions about what makes groups grow and thrive. These surprises include:

- Who owns a thriving group—chapter 1.
- How group evangelism works—chapter 2.
- What makes a great group leader—chapter 3.
- How community influences evangelism—chapter 4.
- How evangelism influences transparency—chapter 5.
- Why worship is central to a group—chapter 6.
- Why it is crucial for a leader to pray—chapter 7.
- How persistence, or lack of it, influences group life—chapter 8.

What surprise(s) got your attention? Feel free to skip around and let your curiosity shape your learning.

What Do You Need to Strengthen?

As you read this book, you will notice places where your small group is not thriving. No group is perfect, but you can make an adjustment, immerse yourself in prayer, and stay the course. God is at work in your group whether or not you see it now.

At the end of each chapter, there are review questions. Take the time to go over these

> *God is at work in your group whether or not you see it now.*

questions individually or with your group to determine what particular areas you need to improve on.

We also encourage you to visit our website (thriving-smallgroups.com) that features a free evaluation tool that will help you determine the health of your group. After completing the survey, you'll find a graph that highlights the strong and weak areas of your group, as measured by:

- Prayer/worship
- Outreach and evangelism
- Care for one another
- Empowering new leaders

Jim Egli has spent twenty years perfecting the research and practical applications you'll find on thrivingsmallgroups.com. The good news is that it's free and will help point out areas you need to work on.

Our prayer is that this book will give you practical and encouraging insights. May your group thrive as you move more and more deeply into all that Christ has for you!

thrivingsmallgroups.com

1
SHIFT FROM MY GROUP TO OUR GROUP

As a part of the leadership in my church, I visit group meetings to support what God is doing in the lives of the leaders and members. Two meetings vividly stand out because of their stark contrast. As I sat in the first meeting, the leader treated it like a mini-church service. He asked the ice breaker question to open but only let one or two share before quickly moving on. After worship, we opened the Scriptures. With a Bible in one hand and a document that looked like a manuscript in the other, the lead-

members of a thriving group take ownership of the group

er proceeded to dominate the meeting for the next 40 minutes. He answered his own questions and even controlled the concluding prayer time. Honestly, I could not wait to get out of there, and by the looks on the faces around the room, I was not the only person feeling this way.

The second meeting was quite a different experience. Actually, I really did not want it to end. When the ice-breaker was presented—not by the leader by the way—everyone shared some quite silly responses. Another group member led us in a simple time of worship. Then the leader opened up the discussion of the lesson. While he was leading this part of the meeting, he only talked about thirty percent of the time.[1] There were lots of questions and interaction. We even stopped in the middle of discussion and prayed for one of the members. Then each member expressed personal needs in the prayer time. At the end, we migrated to the kitchen for refreshment and talked for another thirty minutes. The leader finally told people that we needed to honor the host and leave because the next day was a school day. Otherwise, I think people would have stayed much longer.

> **Leaders don't have to do everything!**

These stories show two totally different group experiences and two very different ways of leading groups.

Shedding the Image of Atlas

According to legend, the mythical god Atlas was forced to hold up the heavens as a special punishment. Atlas couldn't give his task to anyone else; it rested on his shoulders and his alone. Sadly, many leaders gladly imitate Atlas and prefer to chart

A gentle hand often guides better then Our Group a restricted one

their own course without the help of anyone else. Individualistic cultures like those in North America esteem those who "pull themselves up by their own bootstraps." They would rather be burdened like Atlas than receive help from anyone.

One leader in Australia told me that she felt no one in her group measured up as she crassly described her members as having mental issues. Everything depended on her because those in the group were weak, helpless, and even dangerous without her control. Like Atlas, she had to hold the group together by herself. No one was qualified to help her bear this burden.

There's another path, however, that works much better and makes groups thrive. Fred illustrates this. He diligently prepared all week for his Thursday night group. Everyone expected he would give an exegetical teaching from the Bible, opinions from commentators, and illustrations.

Actually, just the opposite happened. Fred spoke very little that evening. He asked others to lead parts of the meeting and to help him lead the Bible discussion. When he did speak, he drew out information from others. Although he had scrutinized the Bible passage over and over, he led the group to dig up the treasures for themselves. He peppered each person with questions that forced them to delve into the text. He placed the burden in the middle of the group and others picked it up.

> **Self-sufficient leaders kill group life!**

The Surprising Discovery: Members Create Thriving Groups

In my conversation with the group leader in Australia, I encouraged her to recognize the Holy Spirit in each member

21

and release them for ministry. She followed my advice and the group came to life. It shifted from her group to their group. After learning how to empower others, she eventually felt the liberty to start another group, knowing that the members were trained and could go on without her.

Thriving groups are characterized by the phrase "our group" rather than Tom's group or Betty's group. Members take ownership for the vision and direction of the group and the leader is the facilitator who mobilizes the members. Life-giving groups get everyone involved because facilitators refuse to do everything. The members own the group and talk about it as their group.

> **The group is NOT a repeat of Sunday morning.**

Thriving groups don't hold up one person as the superstar. The members are not looking at Joe or Tammy to do everything. The group experience is not a repeat of the Sunday morning experience where one person preaches and others sit and listen. Rather, the members experience the freedom to minister to one another. People sit in circles, not at long tables or in opposing lines. They talk to each other and allow the Spirit to work in their midst.

We questioned group leaders to understand how much they empowered members as opposed to doing everything themselves. Those leaders who actively engage their members, delegate responsibility, and instill the "our group" mentality were far more likely to produce new leaders and new groups than domineering and controlling leaders produce, as the graph below indicates.

Facilitator describes the leader's role of empowering each member to develop and grow. Synonyms for empowerment in-

Thriving Groups
Produce More Leaders

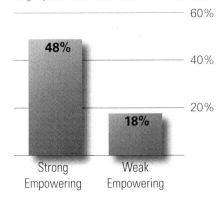

% of groups that have sent out at least one new leader

clude enablement, permission, and approval. Facilitators encourage people to step out, attempt new things, and even embrace the idea of making mistakes while they share, use their gifts, and contribute to the life of the group.

When facilitators leave the group, members have the confidence to continue the group through the help of the Holy Spirit. Above all else, the members have learned to depend on God.

When Brent first stepped into the home group, he was a mess—fearful, nervous, and self-conscious. He was not accustomed to communicating with others and felt like he had little to share. Over the years of sitting in church on Sunday, he had become conditioned to sit, hear, nod his head, talk to a few people after the church worship service, and then go home. He loved Jesus but had little community and interaction with others.

When he first joined the group, everyone noticed his hesitancy. But they loved him, encouraged him, and told him to relax and enjoy himself. Weeks and months passed. Brent soon realized he was in a band of like-minded believers who loved him and had his best interests at heart. He could be transparent with them without feeling judged. The group encouraged him to participate and his confidence grew. Soon he was leading

> **Groups that involve everyone don't have a problem keeping their people.**

the different parts of the group meeting and even the lesson itself. It became apparent that Brent had a gift of teaching and often used it when shar-

ing. Brent even learned to share his faith as the group went out into the community to pray with those who had needs. Brent rarely missed a meeting and even showed up early. The group became a second family to Brent, and in many ways, a more intimate family.

Groups that involve everyone don't have a problem keeping their people. Like Brent, the members don't want to miss even a single meeting. The group becomes their family because they are loved and accepted for who they are. As the graph below shows, these groups are able to keep their people because those attending feel at home.

Empowering Others Adds Members

% of groups that have added 4 or more new members

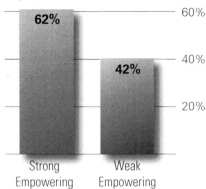

Even the newcomers are soon talking about "our group." One reason is because the facilitator is quick to ask, "what do the rest of you think?" knowing that thriving groups move forward as a team, in unity, and oneness of purpose. The fact is: people want to be a part of "our" group, not "your" group.

Nobody on the Sidelines

In our research, we found that one statement correlated with unhealthy groups: "I like to lead the entire small group meeting myself." This is a death warrant for small groups. It turns members into passive hearers, expecting them to sit in yet another meeting. The leader

> *The reality is that there's too much work for one leader to do alone.*

grows as he or she ministers, but the hearers don't have a chance to exercise their spiritual muscles. But when the group shifts to our group, everyone takes ownership and works to help the group thrive and grow. This takes time, prayer, and effort.

The reality is that there's too much work for one leader to do alone. Consider the pressures that a small group leader places upon himself when he embraces the statement "I need to do all the work."

- Prepare and facilitate all the various parts of the weekly meetings, making it look very polished and professional.
- Personally reach all lost friends for Christ.
- Meet with everyone in the group as often as possible to mentor and disciple them into strong believers.
- Train an intern or apprentice by having them watch what

you do so that when he has his own group, he'll know what to do.

Those who empower members prepare the members to actively participate, be part of a leadership team, and eventually be part of a new small group. They understand that the small group is an excellent place to prepare disciples who make disciples. They are not afraid to ask Mary to lead the ice-breaker or to invite Jim to lead worship. Eventually, they liberate others to facilitate the lesson. They know that people learn best "on the job," so they joyfully allow members to get involved.

Kim and Kim Cole (yes, both husband and wife have the same names!) love small groups and have been part of a church in Pennsylvania that has been small-group focused since the late 1980s. I heard so much about this couple from the lead pastor that I assumed they must be dynamic, talented, and very gifted.

When we met, I was surprised to notice how unassuming they were. They shied away from public leadership roles and were certainly not the superstar types. They freely shared their weaknesses and struggles with their small groups. I've had the privilege to talk with the Coles on different occasions and even attended their group meetings twice.

> *They freely shared their weaknesses and struggles with their small groups.*

The Coles encouraged others to become active participants. They ask each member to lead the ice-breaker, worship, and lesson. They alternate among the willing members, encouraging each person to practice every aspect of group life. They even rotate the host homes among willing members, wanting to give each person the opportunity to practice the blessing of hospitality. The Coles simply participate like the rest of the group and stay mostly behind the scenes.

In contrast, some leaders set themselves up as the Bible answer man or woman. No one else knows quite as much biblical truth as they do. The group turns into a study time. Members are expected to sit and listen. I visited one group in which the leader rattled off numerous Greek words. "Is she trying to impress me with her knowledge?" I thought to myself. I noticed a few thick commentaries on the floor, and she liberally quoted them, teaching 90 percent of the lesson. When others dared to comment, she hesitantly acknowledged them. Quickly, however, she cut them off, preferring her own authoritative voice.

Some pastors actually promote this practice as they hang educational nooses on their lay people, expecting them to go through long periods of ed-

> *Potential leaders cannot be "perfected" before they're sent to do ministry.*

ucation before leading or even ministering in a small group. This approach has two fatal errors. First, it fails to acknowledge that the best learning is caught, not taught. Learning to lead is a process, so potential leaders cannot be "perfected" before they're sent to do ministry. Leaders gain vital experience as they make mistakes, reflect on them, and chart mid-course corrections. The small group is the perfect laboratory for developing leadership.

The second flaw concerns the work of the Holy Spirit. A philosophy that relies on formal training for small group leadership often minimizes the power of, and the reliance on, the Holy Spirit. Take the example of the apostle Paul. During the first century, Paul established churches throughout the Mediterranean and left them in the hands of relatively new Christians.[2] Why? He trusted the Holy Spirit to work through these young leaders.

The Way Jesus Empowered

Jesus taught the multitude but spent the majority of the time ministering to his disciples. This might seem counterintuitive. Why not spend the most time with the most people? Why prioritize a group of twelve? Jesus knew that interactive, quality time with the few would ensure that his movement continue after he left. Teaching them in a crowd while they sat and listened was not sufficient to fully prepare them. He needed them to participate and learn from their experiences. This is how empowered Christians are formed.

> *Quality time with the few ensured that Jesus' movement would continue after he left.*

Jesus didn't simply teach his disciples about prayer. Rather, he empowered them to pray by allowing them to see him in practice. When the disciples finally asked him what he was doing, he seized upon the opportunity to teach them about prayer (Lk. 11:1-4). Instead of offering a class on hermeneutics or exegesis, Jesus quoted Scripture in his dialogue and then explained the Scripture's meaning to them (66 references to the Old Testament in his dialogue with the disciples).

The same is true with evangelism. Jesus evangelized people in the presence of his disciples and then instructed them afterwards. He sent them forth to apply what he taught them. On one occasion the disciples reported to Jesus about their evangelism tour, "Lord, even the demons submit to us in your name" (Lk.10:17). Jesus seized the opportunity to instruct them further and to offer further guidelines: ". . . do not rejoice that the spirits submit to you, but rejoice that your names are written in heaven" (Lk.10:20). Christ knew that theoretical information separated from practical experience would have little lasting value.

Christ was constantly reviewing the experiences of his disciples and then offering additional commentary (Mk. 9:17-29; 6:30-44). His pattern was to:

• Give the disciples experiences and allow them to make personal observations.
• Use the experiences and observations as a starting point to teach a lesson.

People learn best when doing, but they must not be left to themselves. They need personal supervision and guidance to carry on with the work effectively.

Jesus chose the small group setting so that everyone would be involved and no one would remain on the sideline. He encouraged his disciples to minister in the homes (Luke 9 &10), and after Pentecost his disciples met from house to house where everyone could participate and use their spiritual gifts (1 Peter 4:9). Small groups are the perfect setting for everyone to participate and grow.

> *Jesus chose the small group so no one would remain on the sideline.*

Empowering your members will create group ownership and turn your group into a dynamic, thriving small group.

Facilitate

Fresh out of Bible school in 1981, I asked the pastor of my home church in Long Beach, California if I could teach a Bible study (I yearned to show off my newly acquired Bible school knowledge!). Every Tuesday night, I gathered a group of people in the small church bookstore to teach them the Word of God. I didn't prepare questions, nor did I expect those attending to participate. I wanted those present to hear what I had to say more than I wanted to hear them. I had not yet learned the value of facilitating.

> **Your job is to kindle participation among the group members.**

Perhaps you are called to teach or preach. Look for opportunities to use your gifts. Just remember that the group meeting is not the place to practice this gift! Your job is to kindle participation among the group members. The small group focus is the personal application of Bible knowledge to daily life. It's a time when confession, inner healing, transparent sharing and renewal happen.

Great leaders function as facilitators who serve the group and empower the members to enjoy God and each other. Rather than lording over the group, the facilitator, with humility ministers to them at every opportunity. The facilitator's joy is to empower rather than impart knowledge.

Effective facilitators encourage group members to speak what's on their minds. They empower the group members through active listening. They realize that an important small group goal is to build up each member through active listening that results in edification.

The facilitator might ask, "What do the rest of you think?"

All members are asked to respond and add new dimensions. After everyone has taken a turn, the facilitator can then summarize the comments of the group.

Facilitators Empower Others

The root definition of "facilitator" is to make easy. The role of the facilitator is to make it easy for others to participate. Communication in a classroom takes place between student and teacher (question-answer). The teacher imparts information while the students take notes. Communication in a small group flows among all members. Elizabeth, a member of the group, feels just as free to direct her comments to John,

> *The facilitator is not passive—but listens and lets others share.*

a group member, as she does to Jane, the group facilitator. Often the facilitator simply observes the communication that's taking place.

The facilitator is not passive—but listens and lets others share. A facilitator interacts just like other group members, sharing personal reflections, experiences, and modeling transparency.[3] Facilitators diligently mine the riches of God's Word for the purpose of empowering the members to discover God's treasure for themselves. They know how to study the Bible, but the fruit of their study results in increased participation.[4]

Facilitators Learn While Leading

Don't wait too long to use your gifts and talents. You can't grow unless you exercise your muscles along the way.

A farmer wanted to enter the world of horse racing, so he

bought a beautiful race horse. Every day he washed the horse and groomed it. He didn't want to exercise the horse for fear of wearing it out, so he used his faithful mule to perform the farm chores. On the day of the big race, his prize horse could hardly move. His muscles were flabby and atrophied. The farmer had no other choice except to enter his mule in the big race.

> **People learn best while practicing what they're learning.**

Don't sit on the sidelines waiting for the big race. People learn best while practicing what they're learning. Some think it's best to wait until they really know the Bible. "You'll never have enough Bible knowledge," I tell them. "Even recognized, highly skilled Bible teachers are continually learning.

Others think they must wait until they're ready to answer any question. "You don't need to answer every question," I tell them. In fact, I encourage this response to difficult questions: "I'm not sure how to answer that question, but I'm going to look into it this week, and I'll get back to you." This humble stance will create confidence between you and your members. During the week, you can study the Bible, read Bible commentaries, and go to your supervisor or pastor to ask for help.

Facilitators Are Not Bible Teachers

Many misconceptions abound about leadership. Many still believe that small groups and Bible studies are the same thing. For many, group leaders are Bible teachers. The reality is that few small group leaders are qualified to teach. The best group leaders are facilitators who transparently share their lives with those in their groups, praying always that Christ will be formed

Humility is the a big difference between an active and inactive group [handwritten annotation]

in a new way within each person.

Perhaps we would be more willing to release leaders if we would remember that a small group leader's task is to facilitate. A facilitator's job description focuses more on guiding the communication process, praying for members, calling, visiting, and reaching the lost for Christ. Facilitators are trained to guide discussions, encourage others, and grow with the rest of the group. The words of Barbara Fleischer clearly capture the role of the facilitator:

> The word "leader" in our common usage often implies a person who stands apart from a group and directs it. A "facilitator," on the other hand, is a servant of the group, a person there to help the group achieve its purpose. . . The facilitator, likewise, is a co-participant with others in the group, sharing personal reflections and experiences and modeling what membership in the group means. Rather than being over the group, the facilitator encourages each member to share in the responsibility for maintaining a healthy and growthful group life.[5]

TEACHING	FACILITATING
• *Provides Information* • *"Fan" Communication, back & forth between teacher and students* • *Points out logical conclusions* • *Written or oral testing of memorized information*	• *Provides an Experience* • *"Circle" Communication, often only observed by Facilitator* • *Conclusions are discovered* • *Feedback—observed change in values and actions of disciples*

Because small group ministry focuses on raising up facilitators as opposed to Bible teachers, I do not believe that it is essential that a potential leader be required to be an expert on Bible doctrine, be a gifted teacher, or even be a recognized leader in the church in order to lead a small group. If a person has demonstrated his or her love for Jesus Christ and if that person is walking in holiness, small group leadership is a distinct possibility.

> *It's not essential to be a gifted teacher to lead a great group.*

Two Essential Qualities of Facilitators

What skills are necessary to facilitate a group?[6] At least two: They're summed up in the great commandments—love God and love your neighbor. All small group leaders must abundantly possess these two characteristics.

Sincere Love for God

Jesus, God's Son said, "Love the Lord your God with all your heart and with all your soul and with all your mind and with all your strength" (Mark 12:30). No one has perfected loving God completely. The key questions are:

1. Are you growing in your love relationship with Jesus Christ?
2. Are you enjoying his love letter to you on a daily basis?

God uses people who are growing in love with him.

Sincere Love for Others

Jesus followed the first command with a second: "Love your neighbor as yourself. There is no commandment greater than these" (Mark 12:31). The time-tested, oft-quoted phrase still rings true, People don't care how much you know until they know how much you care. Your success as a group leader depends on your love

> *Your success as a group leader depends on your love for the group members.*

for the group members. More than anything else, God uses leaders who care. Anyone can successfully lead a small group—if he or she loves God and is willing to love people.[7]

Develop a Team

I was born and raised in Long Beach, California, which is part of greater Los Angeles. My dad would occasionally take me and my brothers to the Fabulous Forum to see the Los Angeles Lakers. I've watched superstars like Magic Johnson, Kareem Abdul Jabbar, Shaquille O'Neal, and Kobe Bryant. Each of these stars excelled in their own way and were a pleasure to watch. They leapt, spun, and overpowered their opponents like Marvel comic characters. Yet unlike those Marvel comic superheroes, they were helpless to win by themselves. In fact, they were mostly defeated if they tried to personally dominate an opposing five-man team. The odds against them were just too great. Each of these stars needed a team to overcome the opposing squad. Even the famous Lebron James can't succeed on his own. He tried unsuccessfully for years to lead the Cleveland Cavaliers to victory but failed each time without a strong supporting cast.

Team leadership was the norm in the early house churches. In fact, every time leadership is mentioned, it's always in the plural (Acts 20:28; Philippians 1:1). Those leading the early house churches depended on each other to make up for each other's weaknesses.

> *Group members benefit from receiving ministry from a variety of people and their giftings.*

When a team, instead of an individual, leads a small group, more people are involved. One can do the icebreaker, another leads worship, someone else guides the lesson, and yet another directs the prayer time. Group members benefit from receiving ministry from a variety of people and their giftings. Here are some suggestions for getting started to empower a team:

- Take turns leading the various parts of the meeting—including the small group Bible lesson.
- Rotate among the members to host the group.
- Get together outside the meetings with members to build relationships.
- Schedule small group planning meetings to talk about goals and direction.

By involving others, the group will become an exciting place of ministry and growth.

From My Group to Our Group

Empowering others to participate in the group requires forethought, prayer, assigning responsibility, and debriefing on progress. Empowering others requires effort. Doing it alone is far easier, at least in the short term. It is easier right now to do everything yourself. However, it's far less work a month or two from now when others are carrying the load and owning the ministry of the small group.

What's more, it just makes the group more fun! And who doesn't want that?

Points to Consider

- What is the main principle you've learned from this chapter? How will you apply it?
- Does the group see the leader as a facilitator or controller?
- On a scale of 1-10, how empowered are the members of your group?
- Describe some ways that your members are creating a thriving group.

2
HOW EVANGELISM
REALLY WORKS

Billy Sunday was the most famous evangelist of the late nineteenth century. A converted major league baseball player, Sunday captivated people by his wild antics. He stood on the pulpit, ran from one end of the platform to the other, and dove across the stage, pretending to slide into home plate. Sometimes he even smashed chairs to emphasize his points. His sermon notes had to be printed in large letters so that he could catch a glimpse of them as he raced by the pulpit. Sunday preached to more than one

small groups open new possibilities for sharing the gospel

hundred million people and more than one million walked down the sawdust trail to receive Jesus (floors were covered with sawdust to dampen the noise of shuffling feet).

Under Billy Graham, millions walked down the bleacher trail because most crusades were in sports stadiums. I've attended several Billy Graham stadium rallies and always wept when thousands responded to receive Jesus. Because of the long and cherished tradition of people like Sunday and Graham, many equate winning of souls with the work of these leaders. They equate evangelism with a gifted person who can attract a large crowd.

Early Christianity, however, did not operate this way. The church of the first three centuries spread rapidly without mass media, large public gatherings, or famous evangelists. The number of Christians multiplied through underground, decentralized house-to-house networks that spread friendship evangelism. In other words, everyone was an evangelist and shared the gospel to friends, neighbors, and work associates. Today, God is moving similarly in countries like China, Ethiopia, and India.

> *Christians multiplied through underground, decentralized house-to-house networks that spread through friendships.*

The Surprising Discovery:
Mobilized Groups Evangelize the Best

We met Kim and Kim Cole in the last chapter. They are not natural evangelists. They don't preach in the open air or gather large crowds. They do, however, empower others and have multiplied their group seven times. Kim the wife, for example, developed a relationship with Crystal, her next-door neighbor, through intentionally borrowing a common cooking pot. Those in Kim's neighborhood are from English and Irish descent and take great pride in their homes. Kim discovered that the best way to enter their worlds was to ask for help. As Crystal and Kim developed a natural friendship, Christ came into the conversation.

Crystal peppered Kim with hard questions about the Christian faith and Kim had to depend on Jesus for the answers. More than anything, Crystal felt God's love and friendship through Kim and eventually started attending the Cole's Life group with her husband Todd. They began to feel part of a new family and eventually received Jesus. Crystal and Todd completed the church-wide equipping track and started leading their own Life group. They are now living the discipleship lifestyle that the Coles have exemplified repeatedly.

The surprising conclusion from our research is that mobilized groups evangelize more effectively than depending on a gifted evangelist. As the below chart shows, those groups who empower others are also the most fruitful in leading people to Jesus. Each person participates in reaching out to new people and makes them feel at home. There is a clear connection between empowerment and leading others to Christ, as seen in the graph on the next page.

People rarely receive Jesus at the first opportunity to do so. They normally

> *People rarely receive Jesus at the first opportunity to do so.*

need to hear the gospel message on multiple occasions through various people. Thriving groups that empower people expect each member to reach out and make a difference, which increases the group's effectiveness.

Empowering Others Accelerates Salvations

% of groups that saw at least one person
receive Christ in the last six months

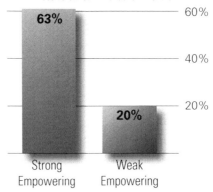

Groups that empower their members naturally attract more visitors. Because members are encouraged to invite their friends, more people actually come to the group. Helping members find their voice is what makes small groups thrive internally and externally.

Facilitators who consistently encourage members to bring friends produce thriving groups that multiply significantly more than groups that do so only occasionally. In fact, facilitators who weekly encourage the members to invite visitors multiply their groups twice as much as those who do so occasionally or not at all.[8]

> *Groups that empower their members naturally attract more visitors.*

Thriving small groups, in other words, empower each member and see more people come to Christ and attract more visitors. The below chart shows the relationship between empowerment and visitors coming to the group.

People invite others to "our" group much more than they do

to "your" group. Why? Because there are multiple entry points in the group, rather than just one—the leader. Visitors build friendships with various people in the group, not just one person. Before they leave, they've been greeted and interacted with group members who have different gifts, talents, and personalities. Some connect better with quiet types, while others seek out the verbal, more sanguine personalities.

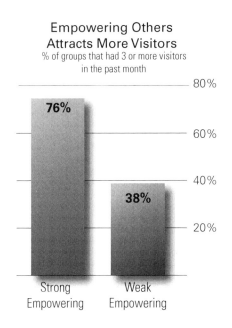

**Empowering Others
Attracts More Visitors**
% of groups that had 3 or more visitors
in the past month

When members feel needed and take ownership for the group, they naturally reach out to others. Members, not just leaders, know what visitors need and how to meet them. Newer members remember their own experiences and can understand

> *Members, not just leaders, know what visitors need and how to meet them.*

the conflicting emotions that occur when entering the group for the first time.

Vivian, for example, was the last person to leave the group's Christmas outreach dinner because she wanted to talk with Carla, a first-time visitor. Vivian herself was a newcomer one year earlier and she knew what Carla felt like. She volunteered to wait at the front door for Carla in church on Sunday and then to sit with her and her husband George. When members feel empowered, they feel responsible to minister to visitors and follow-up as well.

Spreading the Net

In Southern California, we have Disneyland, Knott's Berry Farm, and Magic Mountain. I've lived in this area most of my life, and I've experienced many of the exciting rides in each of these parks—including some of the most exhilarating roller coasters in the world.

The journey of the disciples with Jesus reminds me of a three-year roller coaster ride. They grew more like Jesus in the process, but it certainly wasn't easy. The disciples went from fishing to following a miracle worker who opened blind eyes, multiplied loaves of bread, and raised the dead. Even though they heard the best teaching from the perfect teacher—the God-man—his teaching about his death and resurrection escaped them (Luke 9:45).

When Jesus died on the cross, their roller coaster flew off the rails. It's hard to imagine how horrendous it must have felt to them to watch him suffer. It even drove them to forsake Christ and flee. However, the ride wasn't over. In three days, Jesus rose again. They could see with their own eyes that Jesus was alive and even a brutal Roman cross couldn't keep him down. And then his teachings began to make sense.

Now it was their turn to do radical things and turn the world upside down. Jesus told them to go into the entire world and make new disciples. They already knew

> *They were empowered to live out what they learned from Christ.*

what strategy to use because the Master had prepared them to go into homes, get to know the householder, watch for divine appointments, and then stay in the same home until all in the town or village had heard the Gospel message (Luke 9 & 10).

Then Pentecost happened and the power of the Holy Spirit fell upon them. They were empowered to live out what they learned from Christ. They proclaimed the good news, started multiplying house churches, and made disciples who made disciples. When persecuted, they blessed and prayed for their enemies. Through their love, words, and deeds, many new converts were effectively assimilated into the church. God still uses the formula of love and friendship to reach out to a hurting world today.

Friends Reaching Friends

One revealing small group icebreaker is "Who was most influential in bringing you to Christ?" Most likely you'll hear responses like my brother, someone from work, a relative, teacher, and so forth. Only a small percentage will mention a stranger.

Few people are brought to Christ by strangers. Those closest to us influenced us the most. 70-90 percent of people follow Jesus as a result of relational evangelism through close contacts.[9] The most natural form of evangelism is the type that takes place through loving, caring relationships.

Few non-Christians wake up one Sunday and decide to attend church. Those who do decide to attend a church service won't normally stay unless they are connected to friends or family.

> *The most natural form of evangelism is the type that takes place through loving, caring relationships.*

Examples of friendship evangelism abound in the Bible. In John 1:35-46, we read about Andrew's relationship to Simon and Philip's relationship to Nathanael. Lydia and the Philippian jailer both led their families to follow Christ (Acts 16:15; 16:31-33). Cornelius brought his fellow soldiers and family members to hear the Gospel (Acts 10:1-2, 22-24). And Matthew introduced his friends and fellow tax collectors to Christ (Matthew 9:10). Relationships are the bridges the Gospel travels to change lives.[10] Effective group leaders proactively remind members to become friends with non-Christians and to develop those relationships.

Scratch Where They Itch

Greg Harris lives in Washington State. He was ready to commit suicide because his wife divorced him. He felt like a failure. On top of that, he was working day and night, trying to repay a debt from his wife's custody agreement to support their children. He became very depressed. Then he was injured and began to drink heavily to relieve the pain. He decided it was time to end his life. Tim, a member of Eastside Alliance Church, saw Greg's need, became his friend and encouraged him. Tim invited Greg to his group, where he eventually found the best friend of all—Jesus Christ.

Tim personally invited Greg to the group because he knew the people would meet his needs and personally care for Greg. They did. The community of people in the group became a family to him and Greg was transformed.

Jesus often met needs before discussing spiritual issues. In the book of John we are told that Jesus healed a paralytic (John 5:8) and only later called him to repent (verse 14). In John chapter 8, Jesus stands up for the woman caught in adultery (verse 7) and extends forgiveness to her, challenging her to change her lifestyle (verse 11). In John 9 Christ heals a man who had been born blind (verse 7) and sometime later invites the man to put his trust in Him (verse 35). These people opened up to Christ after He had shown them practical love and had let God display His power.

In the same way, our witness to different people will begin in different ways. Like Jesus we should start at their point of need

> **Jesus often met needs before discussing spiritual issues.**

and continue from there to tell them about the Savior. Pastor David Cho, founder of Yoido Full Gospel Church with some 25,000 small groups, explains Christ's advice about meeting needs:

I tell my cell leaders, 'Don't tell people about Jesus Christ right away when you meet them. First visit them and become their friend, supply their needs and love them.' Right away the neighbors will feel the Christian love and will say, 'Why are you doing this?' They can answer, 'We belong to Yoido Full Gospel Church, and have our own cell group here, and we love you. Why don't you come and attend one of our meetings?'[11]

One important reason Yoido Full Gospel Church has become the largest church in the history of Christianity is because their groups pinpoint those with needs throughout Seoul, South Korea and increasingly throughout the world.

Invite Those Whom God has Placed in Your Life

God has placed your home in a strategic place and in a certain neighborhood. He's given you specific friends. As you reach out to unbelievers, you'll make an exciting discovery: The Holy Spirit has arrived ahead of you! He has given your friends and colleagues a hunger for Christ and has been preparing their hearts. Keep in mind that often you will be just one link in a chain of seed-sowers. Research shows that, on average, a person hears the Gospel seven times before responding to it. When you share your testimony or invite someone to a small group or church and they don't respond to Christ, realize they might need more time. Because most people need to hear the Gospel several times, it's important to provide different opportunities for them to hear the message.

> *Like Jesus we should start at their point of need and continue from there to tell them about the Savior.*

As you look for signs of the Holy Spirit working in your friends' lives, also notice the lives of those close to them. Many times a relative or friend of the person you are ministering to is close to responding to Christ. This person may be the key to unlocking the heart of your friend and many others in that network of relationships. Let God open your eyes to how He's working in the lives you are touching.

Frequently, a non-Christian is hesitant to immediately enter a Sunday worship service. It's much easier to first participate in a group in the warmth of a home. Dale Galloway writes, "Many people who will not attend a church because it is too threatening, will come to a home meeting."[12] Later, these same non-Christians will go to church with a friend they've met in the small group. These natural webs of relationships that start in the small group continue throughout the discipleship process.[13]

> *On average, a person hears the Gospel seven times before responding to it.*

Don't Forget to Pray

I planted an inner-city church in Long Beach, California and pastored it for five years. Many in the congregation were African-Americans. One Sunday morning, I related a fictional story of an African-American lady on the west side of Long Beach who lived alone in her apartment.

The landlord did not care about the tenants and allowed the building to decay. This poor widow did not have any heat in her apartment during the winter months. She decided to take the matter to court. Even though she knew nothing about the court system, she went ahead and filed a complaint anyway.

Unfortunately, her case appeared before a prejudiced, atheistic judge. He thought that African-Americans should be put in their place. In fact, when she first appeared before him, he avoided eye contact while shuffling "more important" papers. However, she came back again and again. She refused to give up even though he became angry. Finally, he became so irritated that he granted her request.

This story helped my congregation understand the meaning of Christ's parable about the poor widow in Luke 18 who refused to accept the status quo.

> **Effective groups and leaders are dedicated to prayer.**

She, too, pled her case before an uncaring judge and won because she refused to accept her unjust situation.

As Christians, we can rebel against the status quo by persistently praying for our unsaved friends to be saved, for the unreached to hear the gospel, and for God's righteousness to reign in the midst of injustice.

Effective groups and leaders are dedicated to prayer. They recognize the most effective tool to win non-Christians to Christ is fervent prayer. They take the words of Paul seriously: "Devote yourselves to prayer, being watchful and thankful" (Colossians 4:2). If we're going to see our friends, family, neighbors, and work associates won to Christ, we must pray.[14]

Salvation often requires a battle. Why? Because Scripture tells us that, "The god of this age has blinded the minds of unbelievers, so that they cannot see the light of the gospel of the glory of Christ, who is the image of God" (2 Corinthians 4:4). Only prayer can break the hold of the enemy. Paul also says in Ephesians 6:12: "For our struggle is not against flesh and blood, but against the rulers, against the authorities, against the powers of this dark world and against the spiritual forces of evil in the heavenly realms."[15]

Group outreach begins with group prayer. My own group has the discipline of putting empty chairs in the middle of the room and praying for those who will fill them. We expected God to answer quickly but it took a long time. Then someone received Jesus in our group, and we rejoiced that God indeed does answer prayer—in his own time. Often it takes longer than we expect because God doesn't work on our schedule (2 Peter 3:8-9).

Prayer will not only open the door for people to be saved but also prepares those in the group to reach out and remember those without Christ. As the group prays, God works in the hearts of the members to contact non-Christians, serve them, and invite them to the group. Some groups have created a "Blessing List," which is simply a piece of paper with the names of unsaved people who are known to group members. Each member contributes one or two names. Then the group prays regularly for the names on the list.

> *Often it takes longer than we expect because God doesn't work on our schedule.*

The facilitator reminds the group members to bless and serve those on the list and to pray that God would work in their lives. As the group plans special outreach events, those on the list are the first to be notified.

Prayer walking is another great way to reach out. Some groups regularly walk the neighborhood to pray for people who live nearby. I recommend walking in pairs through a specific community, praying for salvation to come to each home or apartment you walk past.

Ways to Pray for Unbelievers

- Pray for your non-Christian friends, family, and associates to come out of the darkness and into the light of Christ.
- Pray for personal boldness so that you will not be intimidated.
- Pray for protection, safety, and trust for the person.
- Pray for receptivity when inviting the person to the group.
- Pray fervently against any attack of the enemy on that person.
- Pray for God to give them a hunger for Jesus Christ, to remove all barriers that keep them from responding to Christ, for God to bless each area of their lives, and for the Holy Spirit to make Jesus real to them.

Evangelize as a Team

Michael Jordan was probably the greatest basketball player that ever played. Early in his career Jordan relied heavily on his own talent and efforts to win games. Yet, as he matured he focused on leading a team of winners. It paid off and the Chicago Bulls won the national championship year after year.

Group evangelism is a team effort. The best leaders mobilize the group to work together to reach people for Christ.[16] In Mark 1:17, Jesus tells his disciples whose trade was fishing, "I will make you fishers of men." But fishing alone on the side of a river with a pole in hand definitely was not what Jesus and his fishermen friends had in mind. When they fished they did it as a team using nets. Their fishing involved multiple people and sometimes even multiple boats (John 21:6; Luke 5:6-7). Fishing with a net is far more effective than with a pole. Christ calls us to work together as we share the gospel message.

The tools of the fisherman—the net and the fishing pole—best illustrate small-group evangelism. Small group evangelism uses the net to catch fish. In every sense of the word, it is group evangelism. Everyone participates. David Cho said, "Our cell group system is a net for our Christians to cast. Instead of a pastor fishing for one fish at a time, organized believers form nets to gather hundreds and thousands of fish. A pastor should never try to fish with a single rod but should organize believers into the 'nets' of a cell system."[17]

> *The best leaders mobilize the group to work together to reach people for Christ.*

Non-Christians can see Christ in the life of a believer but can see Him even more clearly through the lives of a diverse and unified body of believers—the small group. God often attracts non-Christians as they see believers related to one another in love. Didn't Jesus affirm this when he told his own group of disciples that by their love the world would believe (John 17:23)?

Rotating homes among group members is an effective way to invite new people to the group. Non-Christians are more likely to attend a group when it's in the house of their group member friend rather than a stranger's home.

Pastor Mark Speeter explains Treasure Hunting at Antioch Fullerton

One form of evangelism is called treasure hunting. The group prays together and asks Jesus to give pictures of people or places to evangelize. One might get a picture of a fountain; another a shopping center; someone else a person in a white shirt. The group then goes out to ask for prayer requests, share the good news of Jesus Christ, and meet needs. God answers prayer and sovereignly connects the prayers and visions with people and places along the way.

- Pre-Outreach:
  - Short equipping – We believe every Christian should know how to clearly share the gospel, yet most don't. Therefore, we seek to train every member in a simple tool like Billy Graham's "Steps to Peace with God."
  - Worship and wait upon the Lord – Worship to connect with God and calm anxiety. After some songs, we will ask the Spirit to give us things to look for and then we write it down. For example: color (orange), name (Frank), item (umbrella and dog).
- Outreach:
  - Word of knowledge: Something specific we couldn't have known. For example, last week on an outreach, some church members got the name "Julio." Within an hour, they met Julio, and he and his son both got saved.
  - Healing – As we do outreach, we ask if they have pain we can pray for. This last week, some church members prayed for a guy with chronic knee pain, and after getting healed, he gave his life to Jesus!
  - Prophecy – God wants to speak unity over people (1 Cor. 14:3).
  - Highlight – As you go, the Spirit may cause someone to "stand out" to you.
  - Gospel – We always accompany God's power with the actual preaching of the gospel, and then incorporating people into the life of the church.
- Post-Outreach: Celebrate and debrief.

More Than One Way to Reach Out

My wife Celyce is great at inviting non-Christians to group outreach events. She uses crafts, holidays, and meals to attract non-Christians. Two neighbors eventually attended her Tuesday group, even though they didn't respond right away. Celyce kept on praying and inviting. One of them received Jesus and started attending the Sunday celebration service.

Special events such as a dinner, picnic, or thematic small group (e.g., one focusing on an issue like marriage, God's existence, etc.) are great ways

> *God often attracts non-Christians as they see believers related to one another in love.*

of reaching non-Christians. On one occasion, a group in which I was involved watched 15 minutes of the movie *Schindler's List*, and then prepared questions on the meaning of eternity. On such occasions, you can invite people because of the special event taking place.[18]

There are many natural ways to build relationships with non-Christians. Birthday parties are an easy way to include both groups at a fun and relaxing event. Other friendship-building activities include holidays, meals, neighborhood parties, and sporting events. Common hobbies and interests are also good ways to bring people together.[19]

Groups with the Heart of Jesus

Jesus showed his disciples how to reach out, heal the sick, and minister to the broken hearted. He then sent them into

Additional ways to empower others through outreach include:

- Party Evangelism – Life Groups throw fun, clean parties in the homes or the city, and invite their friends.
- Service Evangelism – Life Groups band together to serve a need in the community, looking for opportunities to serve alongside non-churched people (Matt 5:16).
- Creative Evangelism – Mark 2 shows us a group that did whatever it took to get their friends to Jesus. Write down names, and think together and come with up creative ideas to do "whatever it takes" short of sinning to get people saved and connected.

homes to do the same. But he didn't leave them alone. He debriefed them on their progress and empowered them to thrive. Christ's band of followers changed the world and pointed the way for the rest of us to empower others.

Empowering members in thriving groups can influence the course of history. Facilitators must not take on the entire evangelistic load. Rather, they should be like Jesus and empower each one to reach out and ultimately to make disciples of all the nations.

Points to Consider

- What is the main principle you've learned from this chapter? How will you apply it?
- How can your group be more effective in reaching unchurched people?
- Do you agree with the statement "Mobilized groups evangelize the best"? Why or why not?
- What can you do to help empower the group to more effectively reach out?

3

ORDINARY PEOPLE WITH EXTRAORDINARY INFLUENCE

In his book, *Einstein: His Life and Universe*, Walter Isaacson talks about Einstein's search for simple, clear formulas to understand the universe. His famous mass-energy formula "$E=mc^2$" is amazingly simple. Granted, this formula is still very complex to me, but for those within the scientific community, Einstein's equation was shockingly straightforward and simple. Einstein had a knack for taking existing truths and proven experiments of other scientists and then bringing those concepts

the best
group leaders
come in
unexpected
packages

together into a simple, unified whole. He possessed an astounding intellect for mathematics and physics.

Jean-François Champollion, the linguist who first deciphered the hieroglyphics on the Rosetta Stone, had a talent for languages. By the time he was ten, he was fluent in French, Latin, Greek, Hebrew, Arabic, Syriac, and Chaldean. He solved the mystery of the hieroglyphics by first learning to speak the ancient Egyptian Coptic language and discovering a connection between the two.

Mozart had extraordinary musical talent. He could write large portions of a symphony in one night and then direct it the next day from memory.

People like Einstein, Champollion, and Mozart have exceptional talents and abilities. The questions before us are: "What are the exceptional talents necessary to facilitate a small group? Is there a particular quality (or qualities) that set apart leaders of flourishing groups and distinguishes them from everyone else?"

Seeing What God Sees

Humans tend to look at visible talents and abilities, and miss hidden characteristics which God prioritizes. Samuel almost overlooked David because he didn't seem like a leader. He assumed that the next king of Israel would be tall, strong, capable, and talented. But the Lord said to Samuel, "Do not consider his appearance or his height, for I have rejected him" (1 Samuel 16:7). God had already noticed a boy with a willing, submissive heart, a

> *Humans tend to look at visible talents and abilities and miss hidden characteristics which God prioritizes.*

boy who could do extraordinary things, and who had already proven those talents by killing a lion and bear (1 Samuel 17:34).

People look at the outward appearance, but the Lord looks at the heart. Samuel was slow to grasp this truth and all seven sons of Jesse passed before Samuel that day, and God rejected each one. Finally Samuel said, "Are

> *God uses people who depend upon Him, not those who depend upon their own appearance, education, or abilities.*

these all the sons you have?" "There is still the youngest," Jesse answered. "He is tending the sheep." Although he was the youngest and most unassuming, he had the most important characteristic: a willing, obedient heart for God.

God tends to use people like David who are fully committed to him. We often assume that leaders must look a certain way, have a specific level of education, and possess the personality of a strong and in-control leader. Yet God uses people who depend upon Him, not those who depend upon their own appearance, education, or abilities.

Surprising Discovery: God Uses the Least Likely

The surprising discovery is that there is no such thing as the perfect leader. All group members should be trained to be disciples of Jesus and in the process of making other disciples. Common thinking is that extraordinary people are needed in effective small group ministry. The truth is that ordinary people grow thriving small groups. As the graph below indicates, those groups that viewed all members as potential leaders were far more likely to reproduce.

Seeing Everyone as a Potential Leader

% of groups that have sent out at least one new leader

Mikel Neuman, a professor at Western Seminary, studied small-group leaders around the world and noticed the same pattern in effective leaders. He concluded that the Holy Spirit specializes in using weak, dependent people. In his book *Home Groups for Urban Culture*, Neuman writes about two leaders:

> They had started three or more groups, and the leadership seemed a bit puzzled. The woman was exceptionally shy, and the man had trouble expressing himself. . . . I was impressed that it is not outstanding speaking gifts that bring a new home group into existence. Caring and prayer . . . are the keys to starting new groups. These leaders allowed other people to participate, recognizing that others had gifts that needed to be used.[20]

It's my guess that the two leaders in Neuman's study discovered the Holy Spirit's energy at their point of weakness—shyness and faltering speech. I've repeatedly noticed that small-group members and leaders who feel weak but cling to God's power are the most fruitful. They realize that apart from God's strength, they have nothing to offer the group.

> *They realize that apart from God's strength, they have nothing to offer the group.*

Throughout this book, I interchange facilitator with leader because facilitation accurately describes what effective leaders do. The word leader often projects the image of someone who most of us are not. Very few feel like leaders, and even those who have visible talents and self-confidence are riddled with a sense of their own inadequacy.

God uses ordinary people who trust in Him. Scripture tells us God has chosen the foolish things of this world to confound the wise and weak things to humble the mighty (1 Corinthians 1:27). We found the same thing in thriving small groups. The good news is that God uses normal, inadequate people. These findings should encourage group members to get involved, knowing that Jesus is glorified in weakness.

Our study showed that anyone can be a successful leader, no matter what their personality or place in life. We discovered that it doesn't matter if those facilitating groups are married, single, young, old, highly educated or illiterate. Nor does it matter if they are male, female, rich, or poor. Personality types have no bearing on leadership effectiveness. Introverts are just as successful as extroverts.

Particular spiritual gifts have no apparent bearing on leadership effectiveness. Leaders lacking the gift of evangelism, for example, are just as likely to have a growing group as those who do have the gift. The gift of teaching also makes no difference in a group's long-term growth.

> *The gift of teaching also makes no difference in a group's long-term growth.*

External, outward characteristics don't make or break those facilitating the group. Rather, it's the inner, spiritual strength that is needed. And anyone can develop spiritual qualities as he or she grows closer to Jesus Christ. Those who trust in Jesus and allow him to supply what is lacking have more power and effectiveness in ministering to others.

One of my heroes is a woman named Lorgia Haro. Lorgia originally hesitated to even host a small group. The leader of the group she attended was moving, and I practically pleaded for someone to host the group while we searched for another leader. Lorgia hesitantly raised her hand, but she shared her own feelings of inadequacy due to her timid nature and the fact that her husband was not a Christian.

Lorgia fulfilled her commitment and opened her house. Unlike Lorgia, we didn't fulfill our commitment—we never did find a leader for that group! In the absence of anyone else to lead the group, Lorgia stepped up to the plate. She asked for the Holy Spirit's strength before each meeting. Her shyness forced her to depend on God's strength, and through her weakness, Jesus used her to love people into the kingdom. The group grew. As she grew in confidence of the Holy Spirit's power, she encouraged members to facilitate their own groups. "If I can do it," she reasoned, "you can, too!" Within the space of seven years, her group multiplied twelve times and over seventy people received Christ. Her husband was one of those converts. Our church grew tremendously because of one weak, shy woman named Lorgia Haro.

Be encouraged! Factors outside of your control do not influence the success of your group. You can't control how old you are, what type of personality you have or what your spiritual gifts are—but none of these things make a significant difference. The differences between successful leaders and unsuccessful ones all relate to controllable behaviors, not to predetermined traits.

Small group leaders should be encouraged by our research. Whether you're male or female, educated or uneducated, married or single, shy or outgoing, a teacher or an evangelist, you can grow your group. The anointing for multiplication doesn't reside with just a few. These statistics reveal that gender, age, marital status, personality, and gifting have little to do with effectiveness as a small group leader. As we'll see in the following chapters, thriving groups depend on simple basics that anyone can put into practice.

All members should be seen as "potential leaders" with the hope that they will

> *The anointing for multiplication doesn't reside with just a few.*

eventually become part of a team. I've noticed that there are far too many "assistant small group leaders" who do nothing but occupy a title. Such a title draped over one or two people often hinders other members from assuming the role of leader. Harold Weitsz, pastor of Little Falls Christian Center in South Africa, echoes this thinking when he writes: "We do not speak of 'group members' any longer, but of trainees to become group leaders."[21]

Granted, not everyone will lead a group for a variety of reasons. But as soon as a small-group system is infected with the thinking that only certain people can lead a group, many believers will become frustrated, forever classified as incapable. The body of Christ belongs to Christ. As facilitators, it's important to commit to train each believer to minister.

God's grace helps all believers fulfill the two greatest commandments: to love God with all they are and to love others like they love themselves (Mark 12:28-31). This means that all of them have the potential to lead a thriving small group.

> *All members should be seen as "potential leaders" with the hope that they will eventually become part of a team.*

All of this information confirms that you can be successful just as you are! God made you special. No one can do it quite like you. God uses the bubbly, the shy, the relaxed, the anxious, and all of the other personality types! Be yourself. It's not a matter of who you are as much as what you do as a small group leader.

God Wants to Receive the Glory

Jesus did not choose key, prominent men to form part of his group of twelve. None of Christ's disciples occupied important positions in the synagogue, nor did any of them belong to the Levitical priesthood. Rather, they were common laboring men, having no professional training, no academic degrees, and no source of inherited wealth. Most were raised in the poorest part of the country. They were impulsive, temperamental, and easily offended. Jesus broke through the barriers that separated the clean and unclean, the obedient and sinful.

Even though they were a motley crew of ordinary people, Jesus invested in them and through them ignited a movement that would reach millions, even billions of people.

Jesus saw hidden potential in them. He detected honesty and a willingness to learn. They possessed a hunger for God, a sincerity to look beyond the religious hypocrisy of their day, and they were looking for someone to lead them to salvation. In calling the despised to himself, in sitting down to a meal with publicans, in initiating the restoration of a Samaritan woman, Jesus demonstrated that even these people were welcomed into the kingdom of God.

> *The disciples were common laboring men, having no professional training, no academic degrees, and no source of inherited wealth.*

One of my favorite passages of Scripture is found in 1 Corinthians chapters 1 and 2. Paul is highlighting the power of the cross of Christ and how God manifested his greatness in an event that is repugnant to unbelievers. Paul says that the wise people think Christ's death is foolish and the strong look at the cross as debilitating weakness. Then Paul goes on to say that God has chosen those who identify with Christ's cross, that is, the foolish and the weak. Why? Paul sums up his argument, "So that no one may boast before him. . . . Let the one who boasts, boast in the Lord" (1 Corinthians 1:29,31).

God chose Gideon to defeat the enemies of Israel in Judges. He might have made a great general in and of himself. But there was one problem. If Gideon defeated the Midianites by his own power, he would have received the glory. So what did God do? He whittled down Gideon's army to 300 men, just to the point where the odds of victory in human terms were reduced to 100 percent impossible. Then God told Gideon to go ahead. And like always, God came through in a miraculous way (Judges 7).

We found that the leaders who were the most fruitful were also the most dependent. They felt weak in themselves but strong in Jesus. Jesus was strong in their weakness, like he said to Paul, "My grace is sufficient for you, for my power is made perfect in weakness" (2 Corinthians 12:9). Paul most likely confronted a physical weakness, but the reason was to keep him from glorying in self, as Paul said,

Therefore, I will boast all the more gladly about my weaknesses, so that Christ's power may rest on me. That is why, for Christ's sake, I delight in weaknesses, in insults, in hardships, in persecutions, in difficulties. For when I am weak, then I am strong (2 Corinthians 12:9-10).

> *Resist the urge to be like Moses, who tried to do everything on his own.*

Some of the best people don't appear to be the best. They are the weakest, fumble the most, and seem the most unprepared. Sometimes we fail to see emerging leadership because we are looking for the wrong things. We often look for those who are like us but pass over those who are not like us.

Practicing Leadership Empowerment

The subtle tendency for small group leaders is to just do it themselves. At times it's easier, more efficient, and even saves time. Resist the urge to be like Moses, who tried to do everything on his own. Moses failed to delegate his responsibilities quickly and ended up with more than one million people clamoring for his attention. Jethro counseled Moses to stop trying to do it all himself and appoint leaders at the grass-root level (Exodus 18). The good news is that Moses listened to his father-in-law and appointed leaders at every level.

Watch the Titles

A title doesn't make a leader—a leader makes a leader. It's not the position that makes the leader; it's the leader that makes the position. Glen Martin and Gary McIntosh point out:

> Some small group ministries use the term co-leader or assistant leader, but this has a negative impact on the multiplication and growth of the ministry in the long run. The problem is associated with the implication that a person can be a co-leader or assistant leader forever. . . . While some may think the terminology doesn't matter, if you are serious about multiplying small groups in the future, the term apprentice is the best one to use. [22]

The deadening effect of placing titles on your group members, while never allowing them to actually facilitate, is well documented. If you've given your potential leader the title of intern, make sure he or she is "interning." Margaret Thatcher, former Prime Minister of Great Britain, once said, "Being in power is like being a lady. If you have to tell people you are, you aren't." Titles have the power to motivate a potential small group leader into action or permanently place them on the sidelines.

> *The deadening effect of placing titles on your group members, while never allowing them to actually facilitate, is well documented.*

Don't Wait Too Long

One young Christian, Fatima, was plagued with a debilitating bone disease but felt compelled to share the gospel as a new believer in her small group. With the zeal that characterized the Samaritan woman, Fatima gathered her non-Christian family and friends for the first meeting. Her house was packed—some arriving two hours early. They listened to the gospel message with rapt attention and in the months that followed, several of them decided to follow Jesus Christ. Fatima's zeal and effectiveness clarified to me the importance of using newer Christians in small group ministry.

One of the most effective evangelists in the New Testament was the woman of Samaria—a new convert of a few hours. Immediately after her encounter with God we read that the woman of Samaria went into action:

> *One of the most effective evangelists in the New Testament was a new convert of a few hours.*

[She] . . . went back to the town and said to the people, "Come, see a man who told me everything I ever did. Could this be "the Christ?" They came out of the town and made their way toward him. . . . Many of the Samaritans from that town believed in him because of the woman's testimony, "He told me everything I ever did." So when the Samaritans came to him, they urged him to stay with them, and he stayed two days. And because of his words many more became believers. They said to the woman, "We no longer believe just because of what you said; now we have heard for ourselves, and we know that this man really is the Savior of the world" (John 4: 28-30, 40-42).

How long did it take the Samaritan woman to tell others

about Jesus? Long enough to go into the village and come back! Don't miss the opportunity of using newer Christians in small group leadership. Jesus didn't; nor did Paul.

Excitement to serve and invite friends is more common in new Christians than mature ones. When they are not allowed to serve right away, they become stagnant and lose their enthusiasm. Our problem so often is not seeing far enough down the road. We fail to connect the person who walks down the aisle to receive Jesus with future leadership in small group ministry. For lack of proper guidance, many potential small group leaders slide out the back door.

> **Most of us would have passed over Mary Magdalene because of her sad spiritual state.**

Release the Willing

Most of us would have passed over Mary Magdalene because of her sad spiritual state (possessed by seven demons). Yet, Jesus released her and used her mightily. She became part of Christ's larger team, and the gospel writers tell us that after his resurrection, Jesus appeared first to Mary Magdalene (Mark 16:9).

John Wesley mastered the art of using every possible leader. Commenting on his genius, Howard Snyder says:

One hears today that it is hard to find enough leaders for small groups or for those to carry on the other responsibilities of the church. Wesley put one in ten, perhaps one in five, to work in significant ministry and leadership. And who were these people? Not the educated or the wealthy with time on their hands, but laboring men and women, husbands and wives and young folks with little or no training, but with spiritual gifts and eagerness to serve. . . . Not only did Wesley reach the masses; he made leaders of thousands of them.[23]

Often the most effective small group leaders are God's treasures that simply need to be unwrapped and then developed. Jesus is all-powerful. He's able to take our brokenness, heal us, and transform us in the process.

FAST People

Dependability takes precedence over ability. Paul told his protégé Timothy, "The things you have heard me say in the presence of many witnesses entrust to reliable people who will also be qualified to teach others" (2 Timothy 2:2). The best facilitators are the most reliable. It's not about talent, education, or any of the other external factors. God wants to develop the internal factors that come from his Spirit. He does that through participation and gift discovery. And this often happens through the hard knocks of failure, picking oneself up again, and pressing on. Look for those who are FAST--Faithful, Available, Servant-oriented, and Teachable.

FAST
F—Faithful
A—Available
S—Servant-oriented
T—Teachable

Faithful: A person might be exceedingly fruitful, but if he or she is not faithful, that person can't be trusted. A large part of fruitful ministry is just showing up, being there on time, and possessing a quality of responsibility—people can count on the person to fulfill what he or she says. Long-term ministry requires faithfulness. It's one of the critical aspects of leadership.

Available: Availability demonstrates priority. In other words, people make time for those things that are important. When a person is willing to stay around a little longer, clean-up when everyone is gone, and volunteer for ministry assignments, it's usually a sign that ministry is important.

Servant-oriented: What kind of attitude does the potential leader have? If the person is gruff, uncaring, and even rude, they are not ready to be the point person on a leadership team. Jesus prioritized the humble servant task of washing the feet of his disciples and warned against lording over others. Possessing knowledge is far less important than applying biblical truths in a way that models the discipleship principles Jesus left with his disciples. And one of the most important discipleship truths is servanthood. Having a servant-heart is an essential trait in ministry.

> *Most of the deep lessons are learned along the way, in the nitty-gritty moments of life.*

Teachable: Completing discipleship equipping is a good place to start, but there's always more to learn in life. Discipleship never ends in this life. Does the potential leader act like he or she has arrived? It's very hard to coach someone who resists counsel and suggestions. Most of the deep lessons are learned along the way, in the nitty-gritty moments of life. It's best not to give leadership positions to those who are not willing to learn and willingly receive correction.

Beyond FAST, transparency and maturity are important traits to look for in potential leaders. Transparency can definitely be modeled and taught, whereas maturity comes over time with experience.

Willingness to Risk

Getting everyone involved in the group does require patience and willingness to risk. Thomas J. Watson, the founder of IBM, said. "The way to succeed is to double your failure rate." This basically means that you are not going to succeed if you are afraid to risk failure, because you will never find better ways of doing things if you are afraid to try something new.

We all make mistakes. Think of the Munich schoolmaster who told a ten-year old boy, "You'll never amount to very much." That little boy was Albert Einstein. Or consider the Decca record company executive who in 1962 refused to give an upstart British rock group a contract. "We don't like the Beatles' sound," he explained. "Groups with guitars are on their way out."[24]

Don't fear mistakes. As Elbert Hubbard said, "The greatest mistake one can make in life is to be continually fearing you will make one." We can learn from our mistakes. Granted, they hurt, but you won't learn unless you make them. A young man, eager

Did you know?
- Babe Ruth struck out 1,330 times. In between his strike-outs, he hit 714 home runs.
- Abraham Lincoln failed twice as a business person and was defeated in six state and national elections before being elected president of the United States.
- R. H. Macy failed in retailing seven times before his store in New York became a success.
- Louisa May Alcott's family encouraged her to find work as a servant or seamstress rather than write. She wrote, and *Little Women* is still popular more than 125 years later.
- Theodor S. (Dr. Seuss) Geisel's first children's book was rejected by 23 publishers. The twenty-fourth publisher sold six million copies.[26]

to climb into the driver's seat of his organization, went into the old man's office and said, "Sir, as you know, I've been appointed by the board to succeed you as president of the bank, and I'd be very grateful for any counsel and help that you could give to me."

The old man said, "Son, sit down. I have two words of counsel for you. Two words." "What are they?" asked the young executive. "Right decisions," said the boss. The young man thought a moment and said, "Sir, that's very helpful, but how does one go about making those right decisions?" The old man responded, "One word: Experience." "Thank you, sir," said the young man. "I'm sure that will be helpful. But really sir, how does one go about gaining experience?" The old man smiled and said, "Two words: Wrong decisions."[25]

Walking on the water toward his disciples, Jesus said, "Take courage! It is I. Don't be afraid." "Lord, if it's you," Peter replied, "tell me to come to you on the water." "Come," he said. Then Peter got down out of the boat, walked on the water and came toward Jesus. But when he saw the wind, he was afraid and, beginning to sink, cried out, "Lord, save me!" Immediately Jesus reached out his hand and caught him. "You of little faith," he said, "why did you doubt?" (Matthew 14:27-32).

> *More admirable is someone who has tried and failed than someone who sits in the boat, warm and content.*

Never belittle Peter for his doubt—at least he was willing to try. I much more admire someone who has tried and failed than someone who sits in the boat, warm and content. Just two chapters later, Peter jumps into the fray and is the first to confirm Christ's Deity, "You are the Christ, the Son of the living God" (Mt. 16:16). Jesus blessed Peter for his reply. Shortly thereafter, with fresh confidence, Peter begins to rebuke Jesus and the Lord says, "Get behind me, Satan! You are a stumbling block to me; you do not have in mind the things of God, but the things of men." Granted, Peter made his share of mistakes. But his willingness to try, and even fail, supplied him with insight that few other apostles possessed.

Never belittle the group member who steps out of the boat and has doubts along the way. Those who try and fail are to be applauded. No one learns anything while sitting in the boat. The key is to fail forward, get back up, and learn from the mistake.

Points to Consider

- What is the main principle you've learned from this chapter? How will you apply it?
- Do you believe that anyone can be an effective facilitator? Why or why not?
- Describe the characteristics of great small group facilitators, as described in this chapter.
- In what area do you need to risk for Jesus?

4

MORE COMMUNITY, MORE GROWTH

I avoided speaking about close fellowship (community) in small groups for many years because I feared groups would stop growing. My first *book Home Cell Group Explosion* highlighted evangelism and multiplication in small groups worldwide. In that book and subsequent ones, I didn't talk much about community, only mentioning that community would take care of itself when people were reaching out.

God changed everything in 2009. I realized while writing the book *Relational*

groups where love abounds reach the world

Disciple that I needed to submit to God's inerrant Word. I saw clearly that Scripture encouraged community and that community might even be considered the most important element in small group ministry.

I realized that Jesus came to establish a new family, and he chose the small group as the way to make this happen. God challenged my thinking and led me to develop a more biblical worldview when looking at small group ministry. Since then, I've fallen in love with the richness of small group community and promote it often.

> *Is community contrary to small group growth? Can the two mix or are they always opposed to one another?*

But the question still lingered. Is community contrary to small group growth? Can the two mix or are they always opposed to one another? Our investigation surprised us and revealed that it doesn't have to be one way or the other.

Surprising Discovery: Groups that are Closer Grow More

As small group coach, I visited Rene and Patty Naranjo's group on many occasions. Their group was always full of people, conversation, and food. No one wanted to leave when the meeting was over. Many of those present played football with Rene the following Saturday. Their group was characterized by rich, close community. Rene and Patty invited long-term friends and maintained those friendships in and outside the group. Their group also grew and multiplied many times. Leaders developed in this atmosphere of love and community.

The surprising discovery is that community stimulates growth and new groups. It naturally leads to outreach, new leaders, and more groups. True community and fervent outreach should not be mutual-

> *When care and love are abundant in groups, newcomers want to stick around.*

ly exclusive. As a group grows in love and unity, there's also the desire to reach out. Community fosters health, vibrancy, and outreach.

The chart below shows how newcomers not only come to the group but also why they stay there. When care and love are abundant in groups, newcomers want to stick around. They feel like they've found a family, a home away from home.

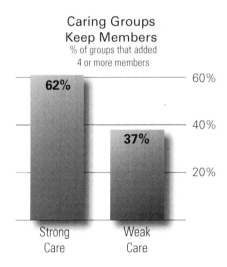

Caring Groups Keep Members
% of groups that added 4 or more members

Think of Christ's group of twelve. There was something irresistible about being with Jesus. His purpose was to help everyone love one another (John 13:34), but we often forget the phrase, "By this everyone will know you are my disciples." Jesus repeats this truth in John 17:21, "That all of them may be one, Father, just as you are in me and I am in you. May they also be in us so that the world may believe that you have sent me." Community and unity leads to people believing in Jesus.

Those who attend caring groups invite their friends. They sense there's something different about the group and about the church. They feel special and wanted. They want to join.

Intimacy Emboldens Members and Future Leaders

My wife Celyce loves people and has been a small group leader for many years. She's also multiplied her group many times. Whenever I do seminars around the world and talk about multiplication, I ask her to share about how she has done it. One thing I've noticed is that she never forces multiplication. It happens naturally. Her method is simple: Love people and help them develop naturally in the group. Part of that process is to

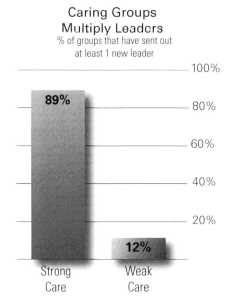

**Caring Groups
Multiply Leaders**
% of groups that have sent out
at least 1 new leader

empower them to lead their own groups.

The above chart shows the correlation between caring relationships and developing new leaders. Where caring for people was strongest, groups were able to multiply more frequently.

Community strengthens the sending out of new leaders because new, potential leaders

> *Community strengthens the sending out of new leaders.*

need a caring atmosphere in which to try, fail, and try again. Mistakes are encouraged and love reigns. Each person feels that their contribution is valued and important. Gift use is high in this environment and members are free to experiment with multiple gifts. Leaders are also developed.

New Leaders Develop Naturally in a Loving Atmosphere

I have to admit that I've forced groups to multiply too quickly in the past. I remember one small group, in which we enjoyed sweet fellowship and community. The main couple who attended the group had a lot of non-Christian friends, booming secular business in the city, and loved the group. Yet, after a certain amount of time, I felt we needed to multiply because that's what small groups were supposed to do. The problem was that it wasn't natural. The community was not deep enough, and no one was ready to facilitate the new group. This couple correctly realized that I was forcing the group to multiply before it was ready— something that I only later realized. They eventually left the group and the church.

Yes, new births will be painful, and discomfort is part of

the growing experience. But I also think we need to make sure that the pain isn't self-inflicted through misdirected motivation and forced outcomes. The emphasis should always be on lovingly making disciples who make disciples and never forget that it's a process that takes time.

People are not afraid to try new things when they feel

> **People are not afraid to try new things when they feel loved and cared for.**

loved and cared for. Christ's own disciples were able to make mistakes, learn in a wholesome atmosphere, and try again. They learned to love one another as they were loved by the Master.

Sometimes Jesus would allow the disciples to make mistakes in order to teach them important lessons and to offer practical application of his teachings. Jesus, for example, allowed Peter to walk to him on the water. Jesus knew he would sink in the process but that valuable lessons would also be learned (Matthew 14:29). The disciples tried to cast out a demon and could not, but later Jesus gave them important instructions about what to do next time (Mark 9:18). The disciples were convinced that Christ would establish his kingdom right there and then, but Jesus taught them about their invisible guide, the Holy Spirit (Acts 1:7-8). Christ's method of discipleship was a constant interaction between hearing, doing, failing, learning, and then teaching new lessons. But love also reigned in this intimate atmosphere and the disciples were emboldened to keep trying and stepping out. Eventually they changed the world as they continued to make disciples.

Jesus molds and shapes those in small groups today. Care

and community among the members is the perfect atmosphere for people to attempt new things, use their gifts, and grow in their confidence to become part of a new group.

Food Builds Community

Picture yourself traveling down a Roman road on your way to attend a first century house church. As you walk down the narrow streets, you notice people everywhere. You're well aware of the over-population of Rome—where approximately one million people live—with the vast majority crowded in one or two room apartments above or behind shops and markets. You finally arrive at the home, which is really an apartment. It's a residential unit with an adjoining courtyard and you notice several rows of apartments connected to each other.

As you enter the home, the rich smell of food fills the air. You notice the food baking outside while you are ushered into the dining area, the largest room in the house. You count thirteen people at the gathering and all have been invited to share the meal together—in memory of Jesus Christ. The story of Christ's last supper with his disciples in the upper room makes Christ's presence seem so real to you. You love the testimonies of changed lives, and people's love for this risen Jesus. You hear stories about those who actually saw Jesus after his resurrection. And they say that Jesus promised to return quickly. Other stories of Christ's miracles are repeated. You love the natural free-flowing atmosphere, the singing, the Scripture reading, and the expectation of the Holy Spirit's presence. And food is central to your experience that evening.

The early church house churches followed the example of Christ who spent a lot of his time on earth eating and fellowshipping with people. The Gospel of Luke is full of stories of Jesus eating with people:

- In Luke 5, Jesus eats with tax collectors and sinners at the home of Levi (5:29-32).
- In Luke 7, Jesus is anointed by a woman in the home of Simon the Pharisee during a meal (7:36-50).
- In Luke 9, Jesus feeds the five thousand (9:10-36).
- In Luke 10, Jesus eats in the home of Mary and Martha (10:38-42).
- In Luke 14, Jesus shares about the parable of the large banquet in which He urges people to invite the poor rather than their friends (14:7-24).
- In Luke 22, we read the account of the Last Supper (22:14-23).
- Even when Jesus is not eating, references to food abound throughout the Gospel. It is safe to say that, throughout Luke's Gospel, Jesus is either going to a meal, at a meal, or coming from a meal.

Jesus spent so much time eating with people that one writer noted, "Jesus ate his way through the Gospels."[27] There's something special about food and fellowship and it really does build community.

> **"Jesus ate his way through the Gospels."**

Eating together has a way of breaking down barriers and warming people up to one another. Jim Egli and I discovered that fellowshipping around food really does build community. Those groups that spent time eating together

86

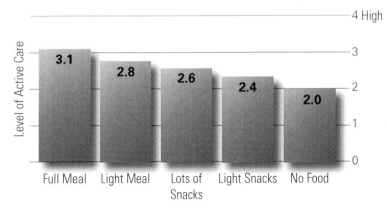

The Affect of Food on Active Caring

also experienced the deepest community as we can on the next page.

Eating together gave groups more community and positively affected the group's health. Eating together is not a magical formula, but it does contribute to community and now we have statistics to prove it.

In 2017, I had the privilege of ministering in Grace Church of Seattle, Washington. Lead pastor Ryan Faust transitioned a 60-year old traditional church to become small-group oriented. All of his elders lead a home group that starts with a meal. My wife and I listened to their stories in a Seattle restaurant, and one theme became clear: deep relationships were forged around the meal.

Eating together gave groups more community and positively affected the group's health.

While in Washington, we visited my daughter and her husband who lead a home group in Puyallup, Washington. They are part of a church that encourages all their small groups to start with a meal. During my time in Washington, I kept on thinking to myself, "Eating meals together plays a vital role in this community." It opens the avenue for communication. Do all small groups need to start with a meal? I don't think so. Is it a great idea to do so? Yes![28]

> *While eating together regularity is important, mindless routine should be avoided.*

We looked deeper into the frequency of eating together, and discovered that while regularity is important, mindless routine should be avoided. Variety is the spice of life and this is true with eating. One week, you might want to have a light snack followed by a full meal. My own group likes to rotate to a local restaurant where we are able to find an isolated space apart from the noise. Some of those attending come directly from work so ordering food works great for them. Discover what works best for you as you try a variety of ways to include food in the group.

Community Matters

God has slowly opened my eyes to the importance of community in small group ministry. It could be the most important way to draw people into a small group today. People increasingly feel isolated in an impersonal society. Children raised in single-parent homes are becoming the norm. And even when parents live together, the sense of community is weak and battered by busyness and shallow relationships.

Jesus offers community to the broken and lonely. He desires that they feel loved in a family setting. Home groups today, just like in the early church, are a wonderful way to demonstrate Christ's new community.

The good news is that biblical community is so attractive that visitors stay, new people are reached, and new leaders are formed. Developing community should never be the primary technique to produce growth. Rather, the attractiveness of biblical community builds up newcomers and strengthens them to the point of wanting to start their own groups. Food plays a critical part in the process, as Jesus and the early church demonstrated.

Points to Consider

- What is the main principle you've learned from this chapter? How will you apply it?
- Community and growth are linked together in this chapter. How have you seen this link in your own group?
- What can you do in your group to bolster community?
- Do you eat together? If not, why not? Plan an activity with your group that involves food.

5
OUTREACH DEEPENS TRANSPARENCY

A few years ago, I encouraged my group to invite unchurched friends to the next group meeting. I was stunned when Judy, a long-time member, said, "I don't want new people in our group. I'm here for the fellowship. I want to be able to share deeply and not have someone new coming to the group. I'm around unbelievers during the week, but here in the group, I want to freely share my heart with people I know well, like all of you." Others agreed. Her words stung because I knew the importance of group

can reaching new people generate deeper sharing?

evangelism, but Judy made a strong point about excluding out-siders to focus on intimacy among our own group members. Was she right? Would inviting new people compromise our deeper sharing and fellowship?

> *Would inviting new people compromise our deeper sharing and fellowship?*

I talked to Judy the next week, reminding her that our commitment in the group was to reach out, and she hes-itantly agreed. Yet her objec-tions stirred me to consider the question, Do closed groups grow deeper in personal sharing and transparency? After all, hanging out with the same people week after week would seem to provide a better atmosphere for transparent sharing. If new people were allowed to come into the group, wouldn't that weaken the fellowship?

Surprising Discovery: Group Outreach Strengthens Transparent Sharing

The four men who attended Jerry's group were faithful and committed. But they also prayed for new people to join them, setting out an empty chair during each meeting and praying for God to bring outsiders to sit in it. God eventually answered their prayer and Carl showed up during an outreach barbeque. Carl, the next-door neighbor of one of the members, was gregarious and engaging. He shared the first night that he had struggled with drugs, but God was setting him free. After attending the group for a few weeks, Jerry said one night, "Carl, you add so much life to our group. You've brought a new, refreshing dynamic, and thanks for coming." Carl not only shared his own struggles but appeared to stimulate others to share more freely.

> *Groups strong in outreach were twice as likely to have strong levels of intimacy.*

But was this an exception? Do groups that reach out maintain deep, transparent sharing or do they drift into superficial communication when new people attend? This is a question that Jim Egli and I thoroughly examined in our research with the question: "Do members of my group feel free to share very personal problems and struggles with one another?" We were surprised by our findings. Groups strong in outreach were twice as likely to have strong levels of intimacy.[29] This discovery goes against our natural way of thinking that says, "Close the doors so we can get more community. Our members won't open up if we're inviting new people and reaching out."

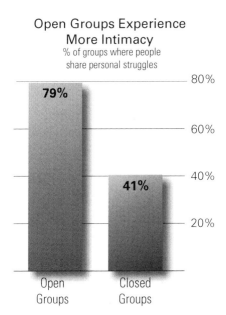

Open Groups Experience More Intimacy
% of groups where people share personal struggles

79%	41%
Open Groups	Closed Groups

As the above graph illustrates, people in open groups feel significantly closer to one another than people in closed groups. In fact, outreaching open groups experience almost twice as much intimacy (79%) as closed groups (41%).

The survey clearly showed that groups actually thrive in sharing more deeply with each other when visitors are present and when outreach is a consistent part of the group's activities. In other words, sharing personal problems and struggles did not happen more readily in closed groups. Just the opposite. Open, evangelizing groups were more intimate than closed groups. The members felt the liberty to freely share while at the same time inviting new people to the group. This chapter demonstrates how reaching out to others strengthens the level of transparency in the group rather than hindering it. But why is this true?

Wounded Healers

Transparent sharing in the small group reveals to non-Christians that believers are indeed not perfect—just forgiven. One of Satan's chief tactics is convincing people that God requires unreachable standards and that only "good" people enter heaven. Small-group evangelism corrects this misconception. Open sharing gives unbelievers a new sense of hope as they realize that Christians have weaknesses and struggles too. The difference is that Christians place their sin and struggles at the foot of the cross of Jesus.

> *One of Satan's chief tactics is convincing people that God requires unreachable standards and that only "good" people enter heaven.*

Dora came to our small group in Ecuador. She felt the liberty to share with the group her doubts about religion. People listened, loved her, and shared their own doubts and testimonies. We encouraged Dora to keep sharing with us and also to go directly to God with her doubts. One Tuesday evening in December, we showed part of the "Jesus" film at our home as part of a special Christmas outreach. Dora was with us, along with other seekers. Dora was accustomed to speaking her mind in the group and felt comfortable with everyone present. After showing the presentation, suddenly Dora cried out, "I'm confused." Everyone was shocked, but we simply loved Dora and cared for her as part of our family.

One week later, Dora received Jesus in our house. God used my wife Celyce to lead Dora to Jesus, but my wife was just one instrument. Dora's doubts stirred the rest of the group to share more freely. People were encouraged by Dora's deep needs and dug down deeper to share their own concerns. Transparent sharing was the key in Dora's conversion and maturation. Our group grew in faith by ministering to Dora, and we all grew in intimacy with one another in the process of reaching out. First Corinthians 14:24–25 brings this out:

> If an unbeliever or someone who does not understand comes in while everybody is prophesying, he will be convinced by all that he is a sinner and will be judged by all, and the secrets of his heart will be laid bare. So he will fall down and worship God, exclaiming, "God is really among you!"

Paul was writing to house churches since literally everyone present was able to prophesy. If everyone could prophesy, it must have been a group small enough for everyone to speak. The word prophesy in this passage refers to "speaking forth truth."[30] Paul was saying that everyone would be able to speak words of truth in light of the unbeliever's needs.[31]

When a person in the small group discloses a need, there is suddenly an opportunity to minister. Spiritual gifts surface. Sharing happens. When no needs are revealed, people often withdraw and turn inward. The presence of people with real hurts stirs the rest of the group to demonstrate care and concern for those who are hurting.

> *The presence of people with real hurts stirs the rest of the group to demonstrate concern.*

Richard Peace, professor of evangelism at Fuller Theological Seminary, wrote a book entitled *Small Group Evangelism*.[32] Peace points out that evangelism in the small group is a natural process. Non-Christians can ask questions, share doubt, and talk about their own spiritual journey. Peace notes, "Our failure to be honest is probably the greatest hindrance to easy and natural conversational witness."[33] This last quote is worth noting. "Our failure to be honest" is a huge hindrance.

Sometimes Christians want to hide their problems to impress the unbeliever with their spotless lives. Perhaps they are thinking, "If I talk too much about my struggles and needs, the unbeliever will wonder if Jesus really makes a difference." The truth, however, is that we are simply one beggar telling another beggar where to get bread. We're all struggling with one form of weakness or another.

Evangelism in a small group does not emphasize a canned,

memorized approach. The gospel is shared in a loving, natural manner through the lives of those who are present. Often non-Christians stay away from churches because they have the mistaken idea that they have to be good enough to become Christians. They have known Christians who failed to live up to biblical standards and have seen phoniness in church members and the Christian mass media. Unbelievers long to know, see, and hear people who are on a journey, wrestling with God each day, willing to talk about things like marriage conflicts, and openness to sharing Christ's power to change people. These same non-Christians are encouraged when they go to a community of honest people who are willing to share their struggles with sin and their dependence on the living God. This type of authenticity often wins unbelievers to Christ.

> _Unbelievers long to know, see, and hear people who are on a journey, wrestling with God each day._

Everyone will face conflict, sickness, trials, and finally death. Unbelievers are looking for answers and probably finding few that satisfy. Satan and this world offer attractive alternatives but most substitutes for God fail and the search continues.

The small group is an exciting place to reach people for Christ. The atmosphere of the home builds caring, warm relationships,[34] and in this context, the facts of the gospel come through not as cold, untested propositions but as living truths visible in the lives of others. People are naturally drawn to Jesus Christ. Non-Christians can ask questions, share doubts, and talk about their own spiritual journeys.[35]

Walking in the Light

Transparency literally means to see through, like transparent glass. True Christian fellowship is not secretive, but honest, open, and free from lies and obscurity. John describes transparency when saying, ". . . if we walk in the light, as he is in the light, we have fellowship with one another, and the blood of Jesus, his Son, purifies us from all sin" (1 John 1:7). In the early house church meetings, each person was encouraged to share freely, as James says, "Therefore confess your sins to each other and pray for each other so that you may be healed" (James 5:16).

Early house churches multiplied throughout the Roman Empire, practicing evangelism and open hospitality. New people joined them, and the house churches grew and multiplied.

As Jesus transformed people, they behaved differently, and friends and neighbors were drawn to this new transformed community. Their changed lifestyles spilled over into the community around them, and at the same time, their intimate fellowship increased. People could see the changes up close as community life was lived out in the open. The home groups were both relationally based but also very effective in outreach. When God is at work both of these things happen. Jesus cultivates a deep love in our lives for one another, and for those who still need him!

> *As Jesus transformed people, they behaved differently, and others were drawn to this community.*

The attractiveness of this new, "called out" society spread throughout the Mediterranean world. When people noticed how lives were changed and how the believers bonded together, they believed the gospel message. Husbands loved wives, slaves were treated with dignity, and married partners submitted to one another. Friends and neighbors were drawn to this new transformed community. The Christian movement attracted people because of the believers' behavior toward one another and toward those outside the church.

God's intention for the early house churches was never to close them off to a dying world around them. Rather, God added new members, and at times, he allowed them to be scattered when they became too comfortable, as in the case of the Jerusalem church. In Acts 8:1 we read, "On that day a great persecution broke out against the church at Jerusalem, and all except the apostles were scattered throughout Judea and Samaria." And what did they do? "Those who had been scattered preached the word wherever they went" (Acts

> *As new people are invited into a group, people get excited and want to share more of their lives.*

8:4). And we read throughout the book of Acts that the early church was a house-to-house movement that celebrated whenever possible (Acts 2:42-46; Acts 5:42; Acts 20:20). As new people are invited into a group, people get excited and want to share more of their lives in the process.

When the group only focuses inwardly on fellowship, it is missing an important aspect of spiritual growth and fails to take the group members to the next level of transparency and discipleship. The very process of small group evangelism brings spiritual growth—not just when someone comes to the group or receives Jesus. I encourage groups, therefore, to pray for non-Christians each week and plan ways to reach out.

Taste and See

My last name "Comiskey" is of Irish descent. When we as a family visited Ireland in 2007, we were eager to explore the area. By far the greatest experience of the trip for me was seeing where Saint Patrick ministered and understanding the impact Patrick had on Ireland. He combined discipleship with evangelism, and his relational strategy started a movement that changed the world.

In the fifth century A.D., when Patrick was about fourteen, he was captured by Irish raiders and taken as a slave to Ireland, where he lived for six years before escaping and returning to his family in England. God saved Patrick, raised him up to become a bishop in the church, and then called him to go back to Ireland as a missionary. Patrick's ministry was so effective that not only was most of Ireland converted, but God used the church in Ireland to send missionaries around the world.

Patrick's model of reaching out to others was highly relational, hospitable, and community-oriented. They lived life in community, but this was never an end in itself. They never lost sight of giving their community away. Patrick and his followers would move into a pagan area to demonstrate Christian community. They took seriously the passage in the book of Psalms that says, "Taste and see that the LORD is good; blessed is the man who takes refuge in him" (34:8). Patrick believed that the truth is first caught and then taught.

Saint Patrick's Celtic movement relied on Christ's own evan-

> *Patrick believed that the truth is first caught and then taught.*

gelistic strategy as seen in John 17 where John tells the disciples that the world would know and believe by their unity. In fact, Patrick's bands of believers talked a lot about the love and unity within the Trinity and used the three-sided shamrock to explain the Trinity. Their honest, transparent lifestyles attracted others to want to follow Jesus and to join their small groups.

Patrick taught that belonging comes before believing. They invited seekers to join their community and participate within it. Those who entered the group saw transformed lives, love in action, and how disciples were supposed to act. The seekers were then invited to become Christ's disciples. As a result of this strategy, many received Jesus, new groups multiplied, and missionary bands infiltrated unreached areas. Discipleship and outreach were intimately connected together.

> *Discipleship and outreach were intimately connected together.*

Saint Patrick started a movement, and he did it by developing relationships with the people and engaging their imagination by using symbols they understood. Many have made comparisons with Saint Patrick's ministry and our own current situation. Like the civilization in Saint Patrick 's Day, people today are hungry for relationships. They want to see Christ among them, become involved in a community, and then naturally grow in their relationship with Christ.

What Patrick accomplished in his day was very similar to evangelism in the early church, where neighbors could see, hear, and taste the fruit of changed lives. The unbelievers wanted change, became believers, and then grew naturally as disciples as they participated in a new community. People saved in those house churches were immediately known to the rest of the members, became part of a new family, were able to exercise their gifts and talents, and ultimately grew to become strong disciples of Jesus Christ.

John Wesley practiced a similar strategy to the Celtic small groups. Open sharing was the cornerstone of Wesley's groups in the eighteenth century. When Wesley died, he left behind a church of 100,000 members and 10,000 groups. Wesley's small groups (called class meetings) normally lasted for one hour, and the main event was "reporting on your soul."[36] The class would open with a song. Then the leader would share a personal, religious experience. Afterwards, he would inquire about the spiritual life of those in the group. The meeting was built upon the sharing of personal experience of the past week. Wesley's class meetings are best described by one word: "transparency."

In Wesley's small groups, everyone was expected to speak freely and plainly about every subject, from their own temptations to building a new house. Within this framework of "open sharing," many were converted. The hearts of sinners melted as they interacted with "saved sinners." Jesus Christ made all the difference.

Churches have spent countless hours trying to figure out how to connect "follow-up" with evangelism. The problem is that step one has been divorced from step two. The relational models offered by the early house churches, Saint Patrick, and John Wesley brought people into the community, allowed them to interact with transformed people, and discipleship happened naturally in the process.

Loving relationships attract people. Jesus told us that our love for one another would draw an unbelieving world to himself. As the church loves one another, people will be attracted to Jesus, become disciples, and then repeat the process of making more disciples.

From Hospital to Healing

2015 was a tough year for my wife and our family. Celyce was in the hospital frequently for diverticulitis and had to have an eventual colon operation. We were grateful for her hospital care, but we couldn't wait to leave. The hospital food was bland, barely edible, and quiet peacefulness was a rare commodity. We all longed for her to heal so we could go home.

The church is a hospital and small groups are the perfect place to find answers that heal. The goal is transformation and healing. When a person or couple reveals a struggle, they are reaching out for help. "Pray for me." "Help me." "We want to stop fighting and start understanding each other," the young couple shares. Such deep sharing springs from an earnest desire to change.

Your group doesn't have to decide between outreach or intimacy. You can have both. Your group will grow *As newcomers join, they will add new life and vision to the group.* more intimate as it reaches out. And as newcomers join, they will add new life and vision to the group. Their stories will enlighten the rest and keep the group from becoming dull, boring, and routine.

Those who have been followers of Jesus for many years will suddenly find new reasons to share their years of experience and exercise their gifts. Those who are new will benefit from that mature wisdom. Everyone will be encouraged and transformed in the process.

Points to Consider

- What is the main principle you've learned from this chapter? How will you apply it?
- Do you feel encouraged to transparently share when new people are in the group? Why or why not?
- Share an experience of someone new joining your group. How did the atmosphere change?
- Transparent sharing helps in the healing process. What can you do to improve the level of transparency in your group?

6

THRIVING GROUPS WORSHIP

Before I spoke to one hundred small group leaders during a Saturday seminar, the lead pastor said to me, "Don't teach about worship as part of the small group order. We don't practice worship in our groups. It's too much of a hassle to prepare the worship singing, and after all, our small groups are primarily for non-Christians."

"Okay," I nodded outwardly, while inwardly wrestling with this new revelation. I understood that a certain number of groups might not have worship, but to

worship, lots of it, brings life and attracts outsiders

exclude worship from all of the small groups?

Some believe, like this particular pastor, that to attract unbelievers, it's best not to appear too Christian and especially to avoid worship singing, which might make unbelievers feel uncomfortable. But is this true?

Surprising Discovery: Thriving Groups Prioritize Worship and Spirituality

One Intervarsity campus group was consumed with finding ways to attract non-believers. The social events weren't working, in spite of all the invitations and planning. Finally, one of the exasperated workers said, "I'm going to bring my non-Christian friend to the prayer meeting tonight." The campus leader was fearful of what might happen. Would the unbeliever be turned off by the reading of Scripture, Christian worship, and deep sharing?

The unbeliever came to the meeting and enjoyed every moment of it. He was thrilled to see people worshipping. He liked the deep sharing. He tasted authenticity, and it was good! As they pondered what happened, they came to see that their non-Christian friends were hungry for God and for authentic relationships. They didn't want the high powered, impersonal programs. They wanted to experience people praying, reading Scripture, and worshipping God.

> **Would the unbeliever be turned off by the reading of Scripture, Christian worship, and deep sharing?**

But is this normally true? We asked those taking the survey whether they included worship singing in their small group. We were curious if including a time of worship would impact small group growth, particularly evangelism. After all, unbelievers don't know Christian worship songs. Does worship singing make them feel uncomfortable and hinder outreach?

A large percentage of the groups said they did include singing and worship (77%). And the groups that worshipped grew faster than the ones which did not. Worship singing positively affects the visitors, and those groups that included worship were also more effective in evangelism.

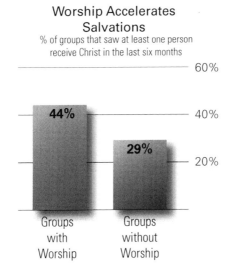

Worship Accelerates Salvations
% of groups that saw at least one person receive Christ in the last six months

From this, we can conclude that worship is not a barrier to visitors, even though they might not be familiar with the songs. Evidently, the presence of God experienced in worship can be felt by these new people and it helps draw them to the group and to Christ.

Groups that thrive focus on Jesus. When people experience Christ's presence and love, they sit-up and take notice. The most effective evangelism lifts up Jesus and allows him to minister

> **Include worship. Bring God into the picture and you'll welcome unbelievers.**

to people. In fact, we recommend including as much worship as possible. Bring God into the picture and you'll welcome unbelievers.

People will join the group because they want to experience God; they have prayer requests and other needs; they are hungry for support from caring people and God. By not including worship, the newcomers might decide that the group is not worth their time. They get social interaction anywhere—a Starbucks, work, or hanging out with a friend. But where can they go to find God? Most likely that's why they came to the group. Don't hide Jesus. Let him be the focus of group activity.

Antioch Community Church, based out of Waco, Texas, began as a youth movement on the Baylor University campus and now plants churches worldwide, focusing on young people whose goal is to reach a lost world for Jesus. All their groups worship God and ask him to minister to those present. One youth group leader described one of her group meetings:

Each youth that walked through the door at the life group was in tears during worship as we prayed over them, spoke prophetic words over their lives, and listened to their hearts. One student's head was healed, another girl decided to give her life to the Lord fully for the first time, and all were deeply touched by Jesus.

Granted, not all groups are as dynamic as this one, but Antioch proactively makes God the focus of group activity so that believers and unbelievers experience his presence.

Jim and I didn't ask how long the group worship lasted. We simply asked those taking the survey if worship through singing is a part of their normal meetings. So how much worship should be included? We advise asking the Holy Spirit to be your guide. Some groups might want to have meetings with extended times of worship. These times might include other elements like taking communion as a group and praying for one another and your community.

> *Ask the Holy Spirit to be your guide.*

God Responds to Heart-felt Worship

Jehoshaphat had a problem. As king of Israel, he was commissioned to protect his nation. Yet, a vast army from Edom was camped on his border, ready to destroy the nation of Israel. Jehoshaphat's immediate response was fear. Yet, he also took the right next step: He sought after God and proclaimed a fast throughout Israel. As the entire nation waited before God, the Spirit of God came upon Jahaziel, son of Zechariah, and he prophesied to those present, "Do not be afraid or discouraged because of this vast army. For the battle is not yours, but God's" (2 Chronicles 20:15).

What kind of battle plan did God give the nation of Israel? A worship plan! The story continues:

> Jehoshaphat appointed men to sing to the LORD and to praise him for the splendor of his holiness as they went out at the head of the army, saying: "Give thanks to the LORD, for his love endures forever."As they began to sing and praise, the LORD set ambushes against the men of Ammon and Moab and Mount Seir who were invading Judah, and they were defeated (2 Chronicles 20:21–22).

God often moves when his people worship. Worship ushers in an atmosphere in which the gifts of the Spirit freely operate. When God's people praise and worship him, God shows up and begins to speak through his gifted people.

I had the privilege of going to Israel in 2011. We toured the ancient temple site and our guide said to us, "We might be standing right now on the very steps where Peter spoke to the multitudes after tongues of fire descended on those in the upper room." I stood speechless. Those passages in Acts chapter two took on new meaning that day.

> *When God's people praise and worship him, God shows up.*

In Acts 1 and 2, we read that those who received the tongues of fire were in one accord in prayer (Acts 1:14; 2:1). They were worshipping God together, and the rest is history. The Spirit descended, people were saved, and a new movement began.

As the movement spread out, Paul went to Philippi to preach the gospel. Both Paul and Silas were severely flogged and thrown into prison with their feet fastened to the stocks. Did they complain and gripe? We read, "About midnight Paul and Silas were praying and singing hymns to God, and the other prisoners were listening to them" (Acts 16:25). God responded with an earthquake and loosed everyone's chains. As a result, the jailer and his entire family were converted.

Groups that thrive focus on God and His glory. Non-Christians are evangelized by the powerful presence of God in the group. Dynamic worship and rich application of God's word convert those who don't know Jesus. Eddie Gibbs says, "But in the heartfelt worship of a people surrendered to him, God is pleased to dwell in the praises of his people. Unbelievers are also likely to sense the presence of God."[37]

In her book *Worship Evangelism*, Sally Morgenthaler calls on the church to consider the remarkable, untapped potential of worship to reach those who aren't followers of Jesus Christ. Morgenthaler shows how to achieve worship that's both culturally relevant and authentic. She often points to John 12:32 where Jesus declares, "And I, when I am lifted up from the earth, will draw all people to myself." When we worship as a small group, Christ is exalted and people are naturally drawn to him.

> **With his presence comes his power and all that we need.**

Talking about the importance of worship, John Wimber, the founder of the Vineyard movement, would often say, "The power is in the presence." Wimber distinguished between seeking God's hand--what he can do for us--with seeking his face—expressing our love and gratitude to him. With his presence comes his power and all that we need. Jesus draws people to himself both in the worship and in the small group.

Wherever Jesus went, crowds followed. They wanted to be near him. They wanted to experience his healing touch and delivering power. They wanted to hear his encouraging words. It is the same today. His presence is the heart of a thriving small group. We must not let anything else become our focus.

Beyond the Music

Worship was always a part of our intergenerational family groups, which my wife and I led for many years. Often my children would lead the worship time, and we loved it. Several years ago, I started leading a men's group that hasn't always included worship singing. I've noticed, however, that whenever we do, people respond with gratitude. Recently we worshipped together with a newcomer in the group. We sang worship choruses with the aid of a YouTube video from Hillsong. Each member had printed lyrics and could follow along. One person was a neighbor who had only been to the group a few times. He appreciated reading the lyrics, singing when he could, and the atmosphere of people singing to Jesus. Before leaving, one of the members spontaneously said, "I sensed God's presence tonight and the worship was very special."

Many leaders feel inadequate to lead worship singing in the group because they think they have to sing like Chris Tomlin or be an expert guitar player. The reality is that God looks at our heart as we sing to him. I've experienced group worship times when the members choked out a joyful noise (with an emphasis on noise).

> **Worship is more than music. It's loving him and wanting him above all else.**

But beyond the singing is God himself who dwells in the praises of his people. And he loves to hear worship and respond by revealing his sweet presences.

Worship is more than simply music. It's loving him and wanting him above all else. Inward motivation is far more important than the outward details. The worship experience glorifies God and tenderizes the hearts of those who are about to hear his Word. Matt Redman's famous chorus rings true, "I'm coming back to the heart of worship, and it's all about you; it's all about you." Worship is all about Jesus.

The Old Testament word for worship literally means to prostrate oneself on the ground—absolute humility before the Creator. Most of the words that refer to worshiping God are used in physical terms: lying prostrate on one's face, kneeling, standing, clapping, lifting up the arms, dancing, lifting and bowing the head.

> Minister "to one another with psalms, hymns, and songs from the Spirit."

In the New Testament, the meaning of the word worship literally means "to kiss." The word worship appears fifty-nine times in the New Testament. Read the book of Revelation if you want to know what God's people will be doing throughout all eternity:

Day and night they never stop saying: "Holy, holy, holy is the Lord God Almighty, who was, and is, and is to come." Whenever the living creatures give glory, honor and thanks to him who sits on the throne and who lives forever and ever, the twenty-four elders fall down before him who sits on the throne, and worship him who lives for ever and ever. They lay their crowns before the throne and say: "You are worthy, our Lord and God, to receive glory and honor and power, for you created all things, and by your will they were created and have their being" (Revelation 4:8-11).

Worship that included singing was common in the early house churches. God gave instructions to the local house churches concerning what they should do. He told them to minister "to one another with psalms, hymns, and songs from the Spirit. Sing and make music from your heart to the Lord." (Ephesians 5:19).

Although spontaneous unplanned worship is wonderful, the best group worship requires diligent planning. The facilitator or member should pick a few songs before the group begins. Print out the words of the songs and then distribute the sheets to everyone in the group. Those who know the songs really well won't need the sheets, but many will need them.

You don't need a guitar player to lead worship. You can create a playlist on a smart phone and hook it up to a simple speaker. Many groups use YouTube to supply background singing while the group follows the words on the song sheets. Simple, quality alternatives-- that don't take too much time and effort—are everywhere on the internet.

The person leading worship should give an exhortation to begin the worship time. "Remember that God is looking at your heart," they might say. "Reflect on the words of the songs while you're singing and know that above all else,

> *You don't need a guitar player to lead worship.*

you're pleasing God." A simple exhortation like this makes a huge difference in the atmosphere.

It's a good idea to allow times of silence between songs and following the time of worship singing. Both during and after worship, allow people to pray out loud. Often in Scripture, God manifested his presence through worship, and it's vitally important to hear from him during this time.

In one meeting, the leader concluded the lesson time by playing worship songs while asking the members to remain in silence as the Holy Spirit ministered to them. The Spirit ministered as the group sat before the Lord. The group left that time super-charged with joy. Several parents who were stressed due to demanding kids and schedules were especially touched. The worship time energized them to serve each other. Dynamic talk and fellowship characterized the remaining moments of that night.

When children are present during worship, encourage them to understand how much God loves them and wants to hear their praises to him. Between songs, ask a child to pray.

Help your group to become sensitive to God while asking him to show you how to reach non-Christians. Put him first in your group, and he'll give you a new, dynamic atmosphere that will edify the saints and evangelize unbelievers.

The key is to allow time to focus on who God is and to thank him for all that he has done. Time spent in worship points people to our faithful and generous God and opens them up to hear him and receive all that he is offering to them.

Jesus is the Power Source

In 1972, NASA launched the exploratory space probe Pioneer 10. The satellite's primary mission was to reach Jupiter, photograph it and its moons and then beam data to Earth about the planet's magnetic field, radiation belts, and atmosphere. Scientists regarded this as a bold plan, be-

> *The key is to allow time to focus on who God is and to thank him for all that he has done.*

cause until that time, no satellite had gone beyond Mars. Pioneer 10 far exceeded the expectations of its designers, not only zooming past Mars, but also Jupiter, Uranus, Neptune, and Pluto. By 1997, twenty-five years after its launch, Pioneer 10 was more than six-billion miles from the sun. And despite the immense distance, the satellite continues to beam back radio signals to scientists on Earth. How does Pioneer 10 continue to emanate signals? The eight-watt transmitter. The key to the continual success of Pioneer 10 is its power source.

Jesus is the power source of effective small groups. Groups that continue week after week without Christ's power are weak groups with little potential for having a kingdom impact. As groups worship Jesus, he will respond, filling the group with his loving presence. The result is effective service to a hurting world.

Points to Consider

- What is the main principle you've learned from this chapter? How will you apply it?
- Do you practice worship singing in your small group? Why or why not?
- How did this chapter connect worship and evangelism?
- What other forms of worship can you practice in your small group besides singing?

7

QUIT STUDYING SO MUCH AND START PRAYING!

Because a school in Texas didn't have a functioning sprinkler system, 200 people perished when a fire burned down the buildings. The principal began to rebuild the school after the initial shock had passed. They called in a leading company in fire prevention equipment to install a sprinkler system. When the new school was opened for public inspection, the principal pointed out the new sprinklers in each room to remove fears of another disaster. The school operated without a problem for a number

pray!
pray!
and
pray some
more!

of years, but then they needed to add on to the existing structure. As work progressed, they made a startling discovery. The new

> **Many depend on the curriculum to make or break the small group experience.**

fire extinguishing equipment had never been connected to the water supply! They had the latest in technology and equipment, yet it was useless.

Small group curriculum abounds today. Endless study guides are created and published each year. Online video curriculum offers ready-made solutions. Many depend on the curriculum to make or break the small group experience. But is it possible for a leader to obtain the best materials and spend hours preparing the study only to see limited results in the lives of group members?

Surprising Discovery: Spiritual Preparation Stimulates Thriving Small Groups

Bill and Tammy lead one of the small groups at First Baptist Church. Bill often comes home from work late and doesn't have a lot of time for preparation. Because his time is limited he is forced to choose between deeper study of the Bible passage or personal spiritual preparation. He assumed that Bible study needed to be his priority because of the in-depth preaching of pastor Gary each Sunday and his ability to quote from the Greek text and unravel difficult Scriptural passages.

The surprising discovery is that time is better spent in prayer than lesson preparation. The research, involving thousands of small groups, dramatically underlines the simple Biblical truth that prayer must be the priority in small group preparation.

Effective facilitators must first connect themselves to the water supply in order to overflow to those within the group. Dependence on God through prayer is connected with people receiving Jesus and visitors attending the group. Prayer is related to all of the factors that make thriving small groups. Those leaders with a strong prayer life were much more effective in leading the group into effective evangelism than those leaders that prayed sparingly.

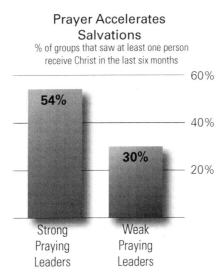

Prayer Accelerates Salvations
% of groups that saw at least one person receive Christ in the last six months

Interestingly, how much time the leader spends studying or preparing the discussion questions made no difference in evangelism and attracting new visitors. The bottom line is this: How much leaders pray makes far more difference than how much they study.

Why does the leader's prayer life influence all dimensions of a small group's life? Why is prayer so pivotal in making Jesus' love real to new people? Statistical analysis usually tells us the "what" but not the "why." In this case, as in most others, we are left to speculate the reasons why. In many small group seminars, we have asked small group leaders themselves why they think that praying leaders have the healthiest and most evangelistically effective groups. They have been quick to offer these possible reasons:

> *How much leaders pray makes far more difference than how much they study.*

- People experience God's presence in small groups soaked in prayer. As we take time with God, his empowering and healing presence is released.
- Group members and guests sense genuine care from leaders who consistently pray for them.
- Christ's joy is evident when people are taking time with Him.
- Praying leaders receive direction from God for their group and their group meetings.

Their suggestions express part of the answer, but perhaps Jesus' own words provide the best answer: "I am the vine; you are the branches. Those who remain in me, and I in them, will produce much fruit. For apart from me you can do nothing" (John 15:5). Statistical analysis says the same thing: fruitfulness results from a vital relationship with Him.

Abide in the Son

Sunflowers derive their name because they follow the sun. When the sun rises in the east, the sunflower will point east. When the sun sets in the west, the flowers point west. These flowers produce a lot of seeds because they are always looking to the sun. When a small group facilitator abides in the Son of God, he or she will bear much fruit, will have wisdom to guide the discussion, and minister to those who are present. Abiding in the Son will transform the facilitator and those in the group.

Peter tells us that God's "divine power has granted to us everything pertaining to life and godliness through the true knowledge of him who called us by his own glory and excellence. For by these he has granted to us his precious and magnificent promises..." (2 Peter 1:3-4a). Paul assures us in Ephesians 3:12 that in Christ "we have

> **Abiding in the Son will transform the facilitator and those in the group.**

boldness and confident access through faith in him." So, when the facilitator needs wisdom, God says he'll provide it. God promises to give wisdom to those who ask (James 1:5).

Some Christians make the mistake of saying, "But I'm not worthy. I've sinned too many times. I've failed him so often. So I can't go to him and ask for wisdom." But that's an excuse for disobedience and unbelief. Every Christian has sinned. Every Christian has failed. Every Christian is unworthy. We do not come to God based on our worthiness. We come to God on the merit of Jesus Christ and his shed blood. Since God commands us to ask him for wisdom, we are disobedient and unbelieving if we do not ask.

Prioritize Spiritual Preparation

I drink black tea almost every afternoon. After boiling the water, I leave the bags in the tea long enough to allow the tea to disperse into the hot water. If I take them out too quickly, the tea doesn't dissolve fully. If I only dip the tea into the hot water, I can barely taste the tea. A great cup of tea is first thoroughly dissolved into the hot water.

Effective small group leaders follow a similar pattern. They don't just dip in and out of the Spirit's presence. Rather, they allow themselves to be fully immersed, so that the Spirit will permeate their entire beings. During the meeting, they have an unseen sense of direction and power.

In our study, we noted that the typical small group leader takes 30 to 60 minutes preparing the lesson, while taking a few moments to pray for the group. In stark contrast to time spent on lesson preparation, a vast majority of leaders (72%) spend less than 30 minutes praying for their group meetings and group members. Here's what we asked and discovered regarding time spent in prayer:

On average, I spend the following amount of time in a week in prayer asking God to work in my small group meeting and its members' lives:	
0-5 minutes	16%
6-15 minutes	28%
16-30 minutes	28%
31-60 minutes	18%
More than 1 hour	10%

What if leaders would spend the same amount of time preparing but shift how that time is spent. It's far wiser to spend most of the time praying instead of studying. It's really just a shift of priorities. With prayer as the new priority, the leader would hear the voice of God, sense his direction, and transform the group in the process. Leaders would emerge naturally because the Spirit of God would control each part of it.

> *With prayer as the new priority, the leader would hear the voice of God.*

In the book of Daniel chapter 2, King Nebuchadnezzar demanded that the wise men and astrologers not only interpret his dream but also tell him what it was. The astrologers answered the king,

There is no one on earth who can do what the king asks! No king, however great and mighty, has ever asked such a thing of any magician or enchanter or astrologer. What the king asks is too difficult. No one can reveal it to the king except the gods, and they do not live among humans (Daniel 2:10-11).

The king was so incensed that he ordered the wise men to be executed. When Daniel heard this, he didn't give up in despair. Rather, he prayed to the Lord of heaven and earth. God revealed the dream to Daniel and the interpretation. Daniel said to the king, "No wise man, enchanter, magician or diviner can explain to the king the mystery he has asked about, but there is a God in heaven who reveals mysteries. He has shown King Nebuchadnezzar what will happen in days to come" (Daniel 2: 27-28).

God is the one who gives wisdom to facilitators as they look to him. He will show them how to lead the group, encourage others to talk, and silence those who talk too much. Effective facilitators rely on the One who knows the hearts of all men and women.

So much of group life is non-verbal and behind the scenes. Some of the most powerful ministry occurs while eating cookies after the meeting. Heart talk often transpires when our guard is down, and we're not worried about every detail of the meeting.

The Spirit might stir the leader to minister to the newcomer or talk with the wayward. He guides the leader to speak to Johnny, who rarely talks during the meeting. Or maybe to just listen, while others lead the conversation. Effective leaders stay in tune with Him, and He makes their way prosperous.

> *Effective leaders stay in tune with Him, and He makes their way prosperous.*

Jesus is our example. He ministered to the clamoring crowds, but he also needed to "close the door" in order to commune with the Father. The gospel of Luke tells us, "Jesus went out to a mountainside to pray, and spent the night praying to God. When morning came, he called his disciples to him and chose twelve of them" (Luke 6:12–13).

Just as Jesus fled from the noise of the multitude to seek the Father, we must also close the door to the crowds of work, minis-

---

Christ's Alone Time

- His ministry began with a forty-day fast in the wilderness (Matthew 4:1–11).
- He chose the twelve disciples after spending the entire night alone (Luke 6:12).
- After receiving the news of the death of John the Baptist, he "withdrew from there in a boat to a lonely place apart" (Matthew 14:13).
- He spent time alone after the miraculous feeding of the five thousand (Matthew 14:23).
- Following a long night of work, "he rose and went out to a lonely place . . ." (Mark 1:35).
- After Jesus healed the leper, he "withdrew to the wilderness and prayed" (Luke 5:16).
- In preparation for the cross, he spent the night praying alone in the garden of Gethsemane (Matthew 26:36–46).

try, and family in order to seek God successfully. We can't really expect to enter into the holy presence of God while sitting in front of the TV, being interrupted by telephone calls, or driving in the car on the way to work.

For any relationship to thrive and deepen, it requires spending intimate time with that person. The same is true with small group leadership. Foundational to growth and effectiveness of leaders is taking time to enjoy God and getting to know him.

The Listening Room

My own group decided to rotate into someone else's home, and I had asked a trainee to lead the group. I dreaded going that night. My mind was in so many different places, and I certainly didn't need another meeting. But the Holy Spirit showed up. Jesus was there in the worship, and everyone could sense his presence. Several people shared impressions they were getting for the group through the gift of prophecy. Praise and gratefulness flowed to God's throne as people acknowledged the Holy Spirit's manifesting himself through spiritual gifts. The facilitator applied God's Word, allowing us to freely answer the open-ended questions. The leader moved out of the way sufficiently to allow for free-flowing conversation. One of the members revealed during the application of God's Word that he and his family were facing a crisis and a possible move to Tennessee.

The leader felt the Spirit saying that we should lay hands on this couple, and God ministered both to them and to us. After a group walk

> *Time in the listening room is essential to receiving the filling of the Spirit and asking God for wisdom.*

around the neighborhood doing prayer evangelism, we shared refreshments together. As I ate a delicious chocolate-chip cookie and engaged in fellowship, I thought to myself, I'm glad I came tonight! When the Holy Spirit is present, he always makes small-group ministry exciting.

Exciting meetings, like the one I just described, happen because of Christ's presence. God uses Spirit-led leaders to guide such meetings, so it's essential that they are filled with the Spirit before the group begins.

> • *Ask for God's filling.*
> • *Confess sin.*
> • *Be filled with the Holy Spirit.*

I encourage leaders to cease all preparation at least one-half hour before the group begins (e.g., lesson, refreshment preparation, etc.) in order to listen to Jesus. Spending time in the listening room is essential to receiving the filling of the Spirit and asking God for wisdom.

The Apostle John wrote, "As for you, the anointing you received from him remains in you, and you do not need anyone to teach you. But as his anointing teaches you about all things and as that anointing is real, not counterfeit—just as it has taught you, remain in him" (1 John 2:27). Effective leaders and members need God's anointing more than any particular study. During this time, I encourage leaders to:

- *Ask for God's filling.* Scripture tells us to ask for the Holy Spirit. Jesus says, "If you then, though you are evil, know how to give good gifts to your children, how much more will your Father in heaven give the Holy Spirit to those who ask him!" (Luke 11:13). Earlier Jesus says, "Ask and it will be given to you; seek and you will find; knock and the door will be opened to you. For everyone who asks receives; he who seeks finds; and to him who knocks, the door will be opened" (Luke 11:9-10).

- *Confess all known sin.* David says, "If I had cherished sin in my heart, the Lord would not have listened; but God has surely listened and has heard my prayer" (Psalm 66:18-19).
- *Be filled with the Spirit.* Of course, this is a daily occurrence but is very important before the group begins. In Ephesians 5:18, Paul says, ". . . be filled with the Spirit." The phrase "be filled" in the Greek points to a continual filling. It's a daily thing.

If you are a small group leader, part of a team, or member in preparation, I invite you to try something this week: Double the time you spend praying for your group members and your group meeting. Invite God to work in fresh ways in each person's life, invite him to draw new people to himself. Listen for any instructions he might want to give you about how to bless and minister to others. We are confident that you will discover what our research has shown: Having a vibrant group depends more on God than on you. Your primary role is to tune into him. Realize that your own relationship with God impacts how others experience him. Here are some simple principles to help you take your relationship with him to the next level:

Be consistent. Consistency makes a big difference. The research revealed that it is important how much time on average people take with God, but it's even more important how consis-

> **Double the time you spend praying for your group members and your group meeting.**

tently they set aside time. Do you daily set aside time for God? What are some simple steps you can take to more consistently connect to God through disciplines such as Bible reading, prayer, journaling, and personal worship?

Be an intercessor. Bring others to God in prayer. Praying for your non-Christian friends, your group members, and your group meeting all contribute to your group's health and growth.

> **Pray for:**
> • *non-Christian friends*
> • *group members*
> • *the group meeting*

How consistently do you pray for others? You might want to talk over this area with a friend or family member. Some people find it easier to intercede with others for non-Christian friends and small group members. Others prefer to weave prayer for others into the fabric of their day, such as when they drive back and forth to work, when they are rocking a baby, or as part of their morning or bedtime routine. How might you pray more consistently for your small group and those close to you who need to experience Christ's love?

John, a small-group leader in Melbourne, Australia, noticed that one of his small-group members, named Mark, had developed a rotten attitude and was even vocalizing it. John dedicated himself to pray daily for Mark, even sending cards of appreciation to him and his family. Week after week, the walls slowly crumbled. One day, John called Mark's office and was told that he was sick and at home. During the lunch break, John visited Mark, praying for him and giving him a big hug before leaving. Mark broke down and confessed his mean spirit and selfishness. He gave John full permission to speak into his life. Today, they are best friends; Mark is even a small group leader now, under

John, and is doing very well!

Through prayer, barriers are broken down and relationships are healed. A new spiritual bond develops that establishes an intimacy and oneness. Prayer gives God the liberty to work in a new way.

I encourage small-group leaders to tell their group members, "I'm praying daily for you." This statement develops an immediate spiritual relationship with that person. The most important gift you can give someone is the gift of prayer.

> *Prayer gives God the liberty to work in a new way.*

It's a gift that lasts and that continues to bear fruit throughout eternity.

After praying for members in private, I encourage leaders to pray aloud for them during the meeting. For example, as Marjorie prays for each member during the meeting, her pastor's heart is evident. Her prayers are so specific and personal, yet she doesn't reveal confidential matters. She warmly lifts each person in the meeting before the throne of God. Marjorie knows her flock, and they are willing to follow her. This type of prayer tells members that their leader cares for them and desires to minister to their needs. It's also an excellent way to model intercessory prayer. Marjorie's example encouraged everyone to pray more consistently. Because she dedicated herself to intercede in prayer for others, she was able to meet the needs of those around her.

Be free. Many twenty-first century Christians feel "too busy" to pray. Yet, the average person spends over 20 hours a week watching television. When we initially began our research, we asked small group leaders how much time they spent watching television on an average day. The statistical analysis showed an extremely strong negative correlation between small group growth and the amount of time the leader spent watching television.

Reconstructing Lives: Edification

The Holy Spirit's ministry is to build up our lives, not tear them down. He's vitally interested in re-constructing people from the inside out. Edification means "to build or construct." Paul wrote to the Corinthian church:

What then shall we say, brothers? When you come together, everyone has a hymn, or a word of instruction, a revelation, a tongue or an interpretation. All of these must be done for the strengthening [edifying] of the church (1 Corinthians 14:26).

The small group is the best place for people's lives to be re-constructed and for them to grow in the grace and knowledge of Jesus Christ.

In the small group, the Holy Spirit challenges and changes people's lives. The intimate atmosphere of the small group makes it possible for this edification to take place. The small group allows each person to share, to minister and to receive ministry from one another. The Scriptures about love and caring come to life in this atmosphere, and ultimately bring healing to the lives of people.

> *The intimate atmosphere of the small group makes it possible for edification to take place.*

Rebuilding the Inner World

It doesn't take long to notice that people outwardly suffer the symptoms of inner wounds. Proverbs 15:13 says, "A happy heart makes the face cheerful, but heartache crushes the spirit." The crushed spirit that characterizes so many is the result of childhood abuse, divorced parents, unforgiveness, resentment, the destructive habits of a parent, rejection, depression, guilt, and various types of fear. There's so much hurt, so much buried anxiety and difficulty, in the lives of people both in and out of the Church.

People need a Savior to touch them and work healing in their hearts. Only God can heal and set people free, and that's why we need inner healing so much. People don't understand the buried hurt that is causing them to suffer so much. But God wants to touch them and set them free. Many find it extremely hard to forgive themselves for their parents' mistakes or their own past decisions. Past issues paralyze present activities and limit future growth. The results include:

- Compulsive behavior
- Self-chastisement
- Doubt
- Feelings of unworthiness
- Denial of what God wants to give them

In the midst of this cultural meltdown, Christ is still head of the Church and Lord over all (Matthew 28:18–20). God has a loving plan for every person, and he longs to heal

> *God longs to heal the lonely, depressed, and disenfranchised.*

the lonely, depressed, and disenfranchised. Jesus not only wants to forgive people of their sins, but he also wants to heal them of their inner pain and emotional sickness. He offers peace in a world full of hurt and despair. An effective small group leader takes advantage of difficult moments to remind members that God is vitally concerned about every aspect of their lives and wants to provide inner healing.

The night that Michael came to my own small group, everything seemed normal. After the lesson on forgiveness from 1 Peter 4:8, however, his need for inner healing surfaced. He shared his deep resentment toward a pastor whom he felt had raped his daughter. Michael had been clinging to his bitterness toward this pastor, which left him joyless and enslaved. That night the Word of God reached deep into his soul, and Michael realized he needed to be set free from his bitterness, both for his own sake and in order to please Jesus Christ. During the prayer time, Michael confessed his bitterness, and the group members prayed for him to experience inner healing. God freed Michael that night from his bitterness and resentment, and he left the meeting filled with joy and peace.

> The small, intimate atmosphere is ideal for healing hurts caused by sin.

The small, intimate atmosphere of the home is ideal for healing hurts caused by sin, the world, and Satan. The leader should remind the small group members of verses like Isaiah 63:9: "In all their distress he too was distressed, and the angel of his presence saved them. In his love and mercy he redeemed them; he lifted them up and carried them all the days of old." King David's reminder of God's love is also good to use in the context of healing in the small group:

> My frame was not hidden from you when I was made in the
> secret place. When I was woven together in the depths of
> the earth, your eyes saw my unformed body. All the days or-
> dained for me were written in your book before one of them
> came to be (Psalm 139:15–16).

The small-group leader can discern the need for inner healing by noticing erratic behavior among members such as: para-
lyzing fear and shyness, lack of trust, confusion, depression, or
compulsive behavior. At the appropriate time in the lesson, the
leader might ask members to share difficult moments when they
experienced pain and rejection in their own lives. The leader
should encourage group members to share honestly and pray for
one another to experience restoration, healing, and a sense of
community.

The good news is that Christ is the Healer. The Scriptures
tell us that "He was despised and rejected by men, a man of
sorrows, and familiar with
suffering" (Isaiah 53:3) and

Christ understands all of the circumstances of our lives.

in Hebrews 4:15 the writer
says "For we do not have a
high priest who is unable to sympathize with our weaknesses,
but we have one who has been tempted in very way, just as we
are." Christ is the only One who is able to understand all of the
circumstances of our lives. The small group provides an excellent
opportunity for people to share times of pain and grief and then
receive the inner healing necessary to live a victorious Christian
life.

Christ's called-out Church should be a hospital in this world. Many wounded people enter this hospital—people who have been beaten up by sin, Satan and all the atrocities that modern life throws at them. Jesus understands. The writer of Hebrews declared:

Since the children have flesh and blood, he [Jesus] too shared in their humanity so that by his death he might destroy him who holds the power of death—that is, the devil. Because he himself suffered when he was tempted, he is able to help those who are being tempted (2:14, 18).

Group Healing

People need to first feel comfortable in the small group before transformation can take place. Wise leaders encourage group members to share honestly and to pray for one another to experience restoration and healing.

> *Encourage each other to share honestly and to pray for one another.*

Effective small-group leaders get members involved so that each person begins to see themselves as God's healing agent. Each member of Christ's body can minister healing to others. No one should sit on the sidelines.

When Monica arrived early to our group, she began to pour out her heart: "I'm so thankful I'm no longer living with Andy. I feel clean inside, but it's still so hard; at times, I feel like I need him." Frank and Kathy arrived in the middle of our conversation and began to minister to Monica from their own experience. My wife also spoke words of encouragement to her, and eventually all of us began to pray for Monica. My wife and Kathy understood Monica's needs more deeply than I, and their prayers hit the emotional nerve center of what Monica was going through.

Monica left that night a renewed person. She dedicated herself to live a pure, holy life—without her live-in boyfriend. Her healing came through the ministry of the body of Christ. Notice the idea of group healing and group community. It's not about one person bringing about all the healing; it's about everyone ministering to one another. It's about getting our eyes off one person and onto everyone involved. Small-group healing is not the preacher's job. Everyone participates, and through the entire group, God moves and blesses each one.

> *Miracles often occur when every member becomes a minister.*

Miracles often occur when every member becomes a minister, and the members of the Church begin to see themselves as instruments of healing. In his book *Connecting*, Larry Crabb, famous author and psychologist, wrote:

Ordinary people have the power to change other people's lives. . . . The power is found in connection, that profound meeting when the truest part of one soul meets the emptiest recesses in another. . . . When that happens, the giver is left more full than before and the receiver less terrified, eventually eager, to experience even deeper, more mutual connection.[38]

The power of small-group ministry is discovered by allowing each member to minister and connect to each other. It's a time when confession, inner healing, transparent sharing, and renewal happen. I love small-group ministry because it allows the grace for everyone to be involved in the healing process. It opens the door for all people to take place in ministering to others and blessing others through powerful healing prayer.[39]

> *Small-group ministry allows everyone to be involved in the healing process.*

Sensitivity to the Spirit

Sensitive small group leaders ask the Holy Spirit to manifest the needs of the members, knowing that the best agenda is the one that meets the needs of those present. When the leader has this in mind, they are willing to do what it takes to make that happen.

I attended one small group meeting in which the leader asked members to pick their favorite songs during the worship time. After each song, the leader asked the person to explain why he or she picked that particular song. One lady, Theresa, picked a song about renewal and later began to sob. "I had an angry confrontation with my husband today. I discovered he's seeing another woman," she blurted out. "I feel so dirty. Please pray for me." The responsive, Spirit-led leader listened to Theresa without overloading her with Scripture and advice. Theresa felt God's love as the leader motioned for her to sit in a chair while the other members prayed for her. Theresa felt cleansed and healed as she left that prayer time. She had come to the meeting bruised and beaten down, but she left filled and encouraged.

The standard for success in small-group ministry is whether or not the members leave the group edified—whether or not healing took place in people's lives—not whether a particular order or plan was followed.

Sensitivity is essential in small-group ministry. Those who excel in small-group ministry are those who are sensitive to needs. It's best to go into the small group prayed up and open to whatever God has for the group. God will guide; He will lead. He'll show the leader what's essential. We

> *Those who excel in small-group ministry are those who are sensitive to needs.*

need to be sensitive to the needs of those who are present. God wants to work in our midst, but we must allow Him to work.

Silence That Promotes the Healing Process

When someone is facing a crisis, it's not the moment to say, "You just need to trust in the Lord. Don't you know that all things work together for good to those who love God, to those who are called according to His purpose?" This advice, while 100 percent correct, will actually do more harm than good to a hurting, grieving person. Before becoming ready to hear advice, the person first must know that God's people will help bear the burden. He or she is longing for a listening ear—not a quick response of an often-quoted scripture passage. Healing takes place in the silence of skilled listening and love. God is the sensitive Healer, and he desires that his people listen to others. Listening is so powerful; it works wonders because it causes people to feel special, loved, and cared for. When someone shares a huge need, it is best to allow for a moment of silence to allow Jesus to minister to that person's needs.

As group members empathize with the person, godly counsel

will ensue: "Joan, I can relate to your fears and doubts brought on by your friend's cancer. When my brother faced brain cancer, I felt those same fears. I wrestled for days, wondering why God would allow this disease to strike my family. But then God showed me. . . ." The scales of past wounds will peel away, and the new creature in Christ will appear as the group ministers through empathetic listening.

It's this shared understanding that is so important; not just one person is listening, but the entire group is involved. When a person is truly listened to, grace and love follows and blesses everyone involved.

It's best for the leader to advise the group to listen rather than quickly responding with pat answers. The small group leader must demonstrate, however, what she wants others to do by her own actions. People won't necessarily follow words, but they will follow actions. Preparing a healing community may take some time, but it's worth the wait. Healing through listening is God's powerful tool to heal a lost and hurting world.

> **Listen rather than quickly responding with pat answers.**

Rebuilding through Encouragement

Listening opens the door for encouragement. Small-group leaders bring healing by tuning their ears for the slightest reason to give praise. If there's even a hint of excellence, a great small-group leader will spot it and acknowledge it. The enemy seeks to accuse each of us through lies that discourage. He might whisper to one group member, "No one respects you. You don't know the Bible well enough. You wouldn't dare make that comment." The small-group leader is God's agent to offer a word of encouragement that will bless the person abundantly and help them to speak up. Praise and encouragement are essential for healing to take place.

I remember being in one small group in which the leader offered a slight criticism to every response. "You almost have it," James would say. When another person responded to the answer, James retorted, "No, that's not it, but you're getting closer." The dance to find the right answer continued. "This is like a high-school quiz," I thought to myself. As James asked the last few questions, the participation ground to a screeching halt. No one wanted to risk embarrassment. The fear of failure permeated the room. A small-group leader needs to listen intently, for healing actually comes in the listening process.

The best small-group leaders view themselves as God's healing agents and encourage all to participate, knowing that encouragement is one of the primary ways to minister God's healing touch. They practice the words of Proverbs 16:24: "Pleasant words are a honeycomb, sweet to the soul and healing to the bones." Great small-group facilitators guard against any information or comments that are not edifying—that destroy rather than build up.

> *Guard against any information or comments that destroy rather than build up.*

One member of my small group had a habit of mixing humor with sarcasm and half-truths. On one occasion, I told the group to stretch out their hands to pray for a person, and that a few could gather around and lay hands on the person. This person said in a half-serious tone, "The Bible doesn't tell us to stretch out our hands; it tells us to lay our hands on people." I didn't know if he was joking or serious, but I did feel challenged, and I felt his comment was not edifying. The Holy Spirit spoke to me to talk directly to him and to share my concern. Because I've told the group repeatedly that gossip is a sin and that the Bible tells us to go directly to the offending person, I needed to model this truth. This person immediately received my words, apologized and communicated that he was only making a joke and meant nothing by the comment.

> *Because sinful human beings are in groups, problems will inevitably occur.*

At times, a small-group leader will need to follow the words of Jesus and privately go to the person who has spoken something hurtful in the small group (Matthew 18:15-17). If what was said negatively affected the group, ask the person to apologize to the entire group. This is one reason that I highly recommend that every small-group leader has a coach. When difficult situations such as these arise, it's great to know there's an experienced leader to whom the small-group leader can share burdens and seek counsel.

Everyone who is attending the small group is in the process of growth and change as well. Because sinful human beings make up the membership of every small group, problems will inevitably occur, but often, careful instruction to the group about the Holy Spirit's desire to edify will set the standard and help avoid problems before they start.

Accountability and the Rebuilding Process

Even after healing takes place among group members, Satan will work overtime to discourage, condemn, and entice people back into a web of lies and condemnation. Transparency without transformation is superficial.

Some people have become experts in unloading deep emotion without any desire or intention to change. In such cases, the healing never seeps down to change core values, but it only resides in the emotional realm. Great small-group leaders revisit areas of confession to make sure transformation has taken place. Satan is a hard taskmaster. He never lets up. Because he hates us and wants to destroy us, he's always attacking and penetrating the darkness of our souls and minds. Group leaders need to follow up on what he has done in the lives of others. Only God can give the grace needed to reach empty hearts

> *Because Satan hates us and wants to destroy us, he's always attacking.*

and minds. We need to be grace-givers, always allowing the Spirit of God to flow through us, ministering to people through the gifts of the Spirit and asking Jesus to take us, mold us, and shape us.

When Vicki began attending a small group from the Verdugo Free Methodist Church in Los Angeles, California, in February 2002, her marriage was falling apart, and her drug problem masked hidden fears. Yet, in the loving small-group atmosphere, Vicki experienced healing and freedom from drugs. Her marriage was restored, and her husband, Tom, received Jesus Christ. Vicki grew in Christ as she shared struggles, received encouragement, and applied God's Word to her situation.

As the months passed, Susan, the group leader, noticed that Vicki was once again taking large doses of medication and reverting back to her old lifestyle. Susan had to confront Vicki with the fact that "when people are scared, they tend to turn to old coping mechanisms. But no matter what old coping mechanisms you turn to, you can't turn away from my love for you." Vicki began to cry, saying, "No matter how many times I've failed, you've never rejected me." Vicki testified that if it had not been for Susan and the group, she would have killed herself the year before.

Susan understood that healing was a process that needed constant follow-up. Great small-group leaders realize that when a person or a couple reveals a struggle, he or she is reaching out for help, saying, "Pray for me," or, "Help me." Victory occurs when true change becomes part of the person's lifestyle. The group should hold the person accountable to improve that behavior—not in a moralistic, legalistic way, but through constant encouragement. There's a certain accountability that must take place, and Susan is a great example of that accountability. As a small group leader, you should hold those around you accountable to what they've experienced. Don't let them go unless they've been healed.

Not all healing will take place in the group environment. Sensitive leaders use the time before and after the meeting to inquire about transformation. For example, a leader might say, "Jim, you shared about your pornographic addiction and your need to break free from that habit. How are you doing in that area?" Even though Jim was touched through prayer, he needs follow-up and constant encouragement in order to remain free.

> Not all healing will take place in the group environment. Use the time before and after the meeting.

Some leaders insist on conducting small-group meetings that are two to three hours long, but if this is the case, people will leave immediately afterward because of their busy schedules. I strongly recommend that a meeting end after one-and-a-half hours to allow time for refreshments and spontaneous interaction. It's often during the refreshment time that the best sharing, evangelism, and community life take place.

Not all community or ministry happens in the group. Small groups are often the springboard for one-on-one relationships that take place outside the meetings. Janet, a member of our small group, silently suffered in her marriage because of a total lack of communication. She wisely didn't blurt out the hurt she carried (which would have maligned her husband to those in the group). She did, however, spend hours with my wife outside the meeting, receiving prayer and encouragement. God ministered to her in the small-group environment but healed her in the relationships that extended from the group.

> *Small groups often initiate one-on-one relationships outside the meetings.*

Healing of the Spirit

The Church is a hospital—not a performing-arts center. Jesus came, in fact, to heal the hurting and needy. He ate with the sinners and hung out with the disenfranchised. He was rejected by the religious rulers because he prioritized the needs of people over adherence to manmade laws.

After healing a blind man on the Sabbath, the Pharisees were convinced that Jesus wasn't the Messiah because he had broken the Sabbath law. Jesus retorted, "For judgment I have come into this world, so that the blind will see and those who see will become blind" (John 9:39). The only ones Jesus couldn't heal were those who failed to grasp their own personal need for healing. Just like a doctor, he came to heal the sick, not the healthy.

Like Christ, the small-group leader should gravitate toward those in the group with needs, offering Christ's healing power to the hurting. The leader must boldly proclaim Christ's desire to heal today—physically, spiritually, and emotionally. The hospital nature of the group is a truism that we must accept: God's healing power is made manifest in the sweet atmosphere of the small group.

> *Gravitate toward those with needs, offering Christ's healing power to the hurting.*

Leaders need Christ-like humility and childlike faith as they minister God's healing power. When this takes place, members will catch on and begin praying for one another, seeing themselves as Christ's agents of healing. The full Gospel will be proclaimed, and all heaven will rejoice at the extension of Christ's bride, the Church.

Back to the Basics

Many believe that John Wesley's class meetings in the eighteenth century saved England from disaster. People were transformed in these groups and holiness spread across England. These home groups followed a very simple formula that all leaders implemented. The leader asked the group the following questions: "How has your soul prospered since the last time we met? Have you fallen into any sin?" The small group leader was trained in asking the questions in different ways. The leader tried to get people involved and help them to apply God's Word.

Today, however, it's rare to even hear about a Methodist class meeting. Why? David Watson summarizes, "Methodists became addicted to curriculum and gradually turned to information-driven small groups."[40] Instead of talking to each other about their relationship with God and the pursuit of holiness, Methodists began focusing on abstract ideas that were increasingly difficult to connect to the intimate and mundane details of their lives. The class meeting became an archaeological relic instead of the vehicle for Christian discipleship.[41] In many Methodist churches today, the Methodist "classes" literally have become Sunday school "classes."

God wants facilitators to prepare their heart and not just their head. It's all about heart preparation. When a person is uncomfortable in

> *Don't be curriculum driven. Rather, be Christ driven and relationally focused.*

talking about his or her relationship with God, a curriculum driven study can be less intimidating. A person can talk about content instead of really talking about a relationship with his or her Creator.

Thriving groups don't allow the group to be curriculum driven. Rather, they want it to be Christ driven and relationally focused. For this to happen, the facilitator must be filled with the Spirit. The facilitator needs to constantly remember that thriving groups reach deeply into people's lives, applying God's Word with the goal of transformation. When preparing for the group, effective group facilitators first prepare the heart. Jesus fills them and allows the Holy Spirit to work in them and through them.

Points to Consider

- What is the main principle you've learned from this chapter? How will you apply it?
- How do you prepare for the small group each week?
- Do you prioritize lesson preparation or personal spiritual preparation? How can you improve your personal spiritual preparation?
- Describe the healing process that has taken place among the members of your group.

8

LEARN THROUGH PERSISTENT PRACTICE

I coached one leader who asked me to guide him to start small groups in his church. After a few weeks, however, it became clear that he wanted someone to give him a 1,2,3 formula for success. "Just tell me the simple, easy steps to grow my church," he said. "I'm very busy and don't have a lot of time for small group ministry." In fact, he asked me to give these so-called "secrets" to his co-worker to implement them while he engaged in other interests. Our coaching relationship didn't last long because I

discover the secret that really is not a secret

151

had no such truths to share with him.

Like many, he was looking for a formula, a magical pill to give him instant success. Those who are looking for quick-fix solutions normally try to find them in:

- the right curriculum
- the right host
- the right leader
- the right homogeneity or mix of people

Thriving small groups, however, don't chase after effortless secrets. They follow a different formula.

Surprising Discovery: Persistent Practice and Adjustments Create Thriving Groups

A man once had a beautiful garden which yielded rich and abundant food. His neighbor saw it and planted his own garden the next spring. But he did nothing to it. There was no watering, no cultivating, and no fertilizing. In the fall, he returned to his devastated garden. There was no fruit; it was overgrown with weeds. He concluded that gardening did not work. On further thought he pondered that the problem was bad soil or maybe he lacked a "green thumb" like his neighbor.

Many look for a formula, a magical pill that promises instant success.

Meanwhile, a third neighbor began gardening. His garden did not immediately yield as much as the first man, but he worked hard and continued learning new skills. As he toiled, he learned. And as he put his new learning into practice year after year, his garden reaped an increasingly abundant harvest.

When considering life-giving small groups, we can't point to just one factor as the key. Rather, all of the ingredients are important. There is no secret or magical cure. Hard work and the steady application of proven principles set thriving groups apart from those groups that simply limp along and barely stay open.

I love the phrase, "The secret is that there is no secret." This phrase reveals that the only guarantee for creating a thriving group is prayer, hard work, learning from mistakes, and persistent practice. Yes, there are ways to adjust groups to make them more fruitful, but balanced consistency wins out over time. Effective small groups thrive because people in them are willing to learn, grow, and persist.

Thriving small groups practice a balanced diet of care, outreach, spiritual preparation, and empowerment. They refuse to look at just one thing to the neglect of others. Those facilitating thriving groups persistently show up each

> **"The secret is that there is no secret."**

week and would be considered FAST leaders (faithful, available, servant-oriented, and teachable). They humbly seek God each day for his direction and make mid-course corrections to improve their leadership. Their groups practice up-reach (worship to God), in-reach (care for one-another), and outreach (focusing on a lost world) in a balanced way.

While there is no one secret, like "just pray" or "just reach out," there are combinations of health factors that produce thriving groups. A well-rounded meeting, for example, stimulates thriving groups, just like the combination of soil, water, and sunshine nourishes plant life.

Balanced Consistency

Some people excel in one area of life, such as career, family, school, health, and so forth. But to excel in all of them requires balance. It's like accomplishing any goal in life. If reaching a goal means sacrificing the marriage, is it worthwhile to fulfill that goal? Or if fulfilling a dream depletes a person's health, is it the right dream?

The same is true with healthy groups. Evangelistic groups are great, but if they're not keeping the people who are won to Christ, the group is considered unhealthy. It's like having a healthy digestive system while struggling with blood circulation or kidney failure. True health means that all the parts are functioning well and that the entire body is healthy.

The groups that thrived practiced a consistent, balanced diet within the group. We asked leaders and members what their groups looked like.

> *True health means that all the parts are functioning well.*

We noticed that thriving groups practiced balanced consistency and focused on participation. Effective facilitators realized that variety is important and refused to allow their groups to exclusively focus on just one aspect of group life. So how can a group achieve balanced consistency? I suggest following the 4Ws.

Welcome (15 minutes)

Most group members are tired when they arrive at the group. They've worked hard all day and probably don't feel like being spiritual. Some will attend because they know they should be there, not because they feel like attending. Be-

> *A great icebreaker stirs members to talk about hobbies, family background, or personal experiences.*

gin on a joyful note. Let them ease into group life.

The Welcome time normally begins with a dynamic question that breaks the ice. The best icebreakers guarantee a response. You can buy entire books on lively icebreakers, so you shouldn't experience a shortage in this area.[42]

Most people know us because of our profession. We're known as a teacher, construction worker, doctor, housewife, and so forth. A great icebreaker stirs members to talk about hobbies, family background, or personal experiences. The icebreaker draws the group together in a family atmosphere.

Some small groups eat together before the group begins or provide a light snack during the Welcome time. People often feel more socially inclined when eating something. Many prefer a refreshment time at the end of the group meeting.

Evaluation Question: When you've finished the Welcome Time, are group members more comfortable with each other and ready to enjoy being together?

Worship (20 minutes)

The goal of the Worship time is to enter the presence of the living God and to give Him control of the meeting. The worship time helps the group to go beyond socializing. Without Christ's presence, the small group is no different than a work party, a family gathering, or a meeting of friends at a sports event. Entering God's presence through song is an important part of the worship time, as we've presented in this book. It's best that everyone has a song sheet because:

- First-time visitors will feel uncomfortable without seeing the words.
- Some new Christians or church members don't know the worship choruses of your church.
- You'll have more liberty to sing new songs.

> **Read Psalms, pray sentence prayers, or wait in silence.**

While singing is important, don't limit the Worship Time to singing songs. The group can experience God's presence through reading Psalms together, praying sentence prayers, or even waiting in silence.

Evaluation question: When finished with worship, is the group focused on God and ready for Him to minister to the group?

Word (40 minutes)

The Word time is when God speaks to the members through Scripture. Resources abound to prepare a quality lesson. One of the best resources is the Serendipity Bible because it's loaded with group questions for most Bible passages.

Many small groups follow the same theme and Scripture of the Sunday message. Even if this is the case, it's best not to discuss the sermon. The people should interact with God's Word, not with the pastor or sermon. If the sermon itself is the reference point, visitors and those who missed the worship service will feel isolated.

Even though the church provides the lesson, it's essential that each small group facilitator examines the lesson and applies it according

> *The people should interact with God's Word, not with the pastor or sermon.*

to the needs in the group. Don't allow your people to leave the group without having expressed the application of Biblical truths to their own lives. I know of one leader who likes to conclude the Word time by saying: "In light of what we've read and discussed in this passage, how do you think God wants to use this in your life or the life of this group?"

Every lesson should give people something to feel, to remember, and to do. The goal of the small group is to transform lives rather than simply gain knowledge. For this reason, it's great to remind group members about last week's challenge and to determine if anything significant happened.

One of the most common errors in small group agendas is including too many discussion questions. Some facilitators feel obligated to cover all the questions—even if there are ten or more. A good Word time has three to five questions. My advice is to let the people leave with a hunger for more rather than a commitment to never return to such a long, boring meeting.

Without fail, God speaks to the group through his Word, and people recognize their needs. I find it very effective to ask for specific prayer requests after the lesson time, making sure everyone is prayed for. If the Word time lasts forty minutes, take ten of those forty minutes to pray for specific needs among group members.

Evaluation questions: Did the group share honestly and manifest vulnerability before one another? Did the group learn how to walk more obediently with Christ during the week?

Works (15 minutes)

The last part of the small group meeting, the Works time (or Witness time), helps the group to focus on others. There is no "one way" to do this. The main thought that should guide this time is outreach. The type of outreach might vary on a weekly basis:

- Praying for non-Christians to invite
- Preparing a social project
- Planning for a future multiplication
- Deciding on the next outreach event for the group (e.g., dinner, video, picnic, etc.)
- Praying for non-Christian families

The leader might ask the group, "Remember to pray for our new multiplication that will begin in two months. Pray for Frank, who needs to complete the last training course, so he'll be ready to start the new group." During this time, you might promote and plan a social outreach project. I'm convinced that small groups are capable of meeting the physical needs of those both inside and outside the group.

Other ideas: Reach out to the community by visiting a retirement home, ministering to street kids, or helping out in an

> *During this time, you might promote and plan a social outreach project.*

orphanage or drug rehabilitation center.

Evaluation question: When we're done, was Jesus working through us to reach others?

Balanced variety and consistency is critical. It's like a car. A typical car will stop functioning if just one of the many critical parts breaks down. If the fuel injection system stops functioning, the car will stop. What happens if the transmission quits working? The whole car will either quit or limp along until the systems are fixed and functioning normally. Empowerment is critical to thriving small groups. But it's not the only critical element. Reaching out, reaching in, worship, and spiritual preparation are all part of the package.

A Life-time Habit

Finding the right balance in small group life doesn't happen overnight. The best facilitators stick with it over the long-haul and fine-tune their leadership over time.

In 2011, I had the privilege of honoring small group leaders in San Salvador, El Salvador. Only small group leaders, coaches, and pastors were invited, but the Elim Church needed to rent a football stadium to make room for all of them!

That night, Mario Vega, Senior Pastor of the Elim Church, handed out plaques to those who had been leading a small group continually for twenty-five years or more. Some thirty leaders came forward to receive their plaques. Some of them were so old they had to be helped to the pulpit to receive their reward. For these people, it would be very hard not to lead a small group.

Hortensia was one of the original small group leaders Mario trained in 1986. She initially volunteered to host a small group in her home. The group in her home multiplied some forty times. After about ten years of serving as hostess, pastor Mario thought it would be good to give her a break. Mario talked to her zone pastor who agreed that she deserved a rest. So the group in her home moved to another house.

But the next day, Hortensia came to the church looking for Mario. She was crying like a little girl and said to him, "Please, tell me what has been my sin to have the small group taken away from me." Mario explained that there was no such sin but only sensitivity towards her for serving so many years as hostess and that she deserved a break. But she told Mario that the group in her house was already part of her life and that she wanted to be a hostess, always.

> **Making mid-course corrections is critical to effective small group leadership.**

She got her group back on the following week. Hortensia was one of the people honored for serving as a hostess for three decades. For her, having a small group in her house is a critical part of her lifestyle, her nature as a believer in Christ. Hortensia is an admirable example of love, passion, and persistence.

Don't Give Up

K. Anders Ericsson, Professor of Psychology at Florida State University and ringleader of what might be called the Expert Performance Movement, attempted to answer the question, "When someone is very good at a given thing, what is it that actually makes him good?" Ericsson says, "A lot of people believe there are some inherent limits they were born with. But there is surprisingly little hard evidence that anyone could attain any kind of exceptional performance without spending a lot of time perfecting it."[43]

Balanced practice, feedback, retooling, and pressing on are the key to small group success. It's not one thing that makes the difference—it's consistent movement forward over a long period of time. How do you know if you're doing a great job? Why don't you ask the group? Find out what they need. How can you get each member more involved? Ask them? Are they comfortable with your meeting place? You won't know unless you ask. Perhaps they would like to do more rotation and even meet occasionally at a restaurant. Getting feedback and then making any necessary mid-course corrections is critical to effective small group leadership.

Jim Collins wrote in *From Good to Great*, "In building greatness, there is no single defining action, no grand program, no one killer innovation, no solitary lucky break, no miracle moment. Rather, the process resembles relentlessly pushing a giant, heavy flywheel in one direction, turn upon turn, building momentum until a point of breakthrough and beyond."[44] Persistence. Determination. Pressing on. This is what effective small group life is all about.

> *Persistence.*
> *Determination.*
> *Pressing on.*

Colin Powell once said, "A dream doesn't become reality through magic, it takes sweat, determination and hard work."[45] The road is not easy, but it's worthwhile because ministering to others in small groups is God's plan, both when Jesus walked on this earth and today in the twenty-first century.

Successful small group leaders keep on doing the things they know they should do. They perfect their leadership through constant practice. They are willing to do what it takes to make their groups successful. In other words, they persist. They learn from their mistakes, make mid-course corrections, and keep pressing on. Their groups thrive as a result.

Jesus in the Midst

The secret is that there is no secret. But if there were one principle that stood out in our research, it would be this: Groups that thrive make Jesus the central focus and make sure he is in their midst. They apply the verse in Matthew 18:20 where Jesus says, "For where two or three gather in my name, there am I with them." With Jesus in their midst, the group thrives.

Colossians 1:7-18 tells us, "He is before all things, and in him all things hold together. And he is the head of the body, the church; he is the beginning and the firstborn from among the dead, so that in everything he might have the supremacy." Only when the group is working in harmony with the head, Jesus Christ, do things run smoothly. As each part fulfills its purpose, the body grows and develops.

> *The voice of Jesus will give the leader words of counsel while ministering to others.*

As the facilitator hears the voice of Jesus, that same voice will give the leader words of counsel while ministering to others. As he confesses and surrenders his weaknesses to Jesus, there will be new power and guidance to minister to others. Paul reminds the Roman house group, "May the

God of hope fill you with all joy and peace as you trust in him, so that you may overflow with hope by the power of the Holy Spirit" (Romans 15:13). Christ's hidden life within will bear fruit in small group ministry and vital growth will take place.

In 2017, we bought two trellises to contain a growing vine in our backyard. Within nine months, the vine branches had covered the trellises, filled up all the empty spaces, and the vine is now growing upward, looking for new ways to extend itself. As the pulsating, thriving life of Jesus spreads from group to group, members will be built up, disciples will be formed, and a lost world will be reached for the Lord Jesus Christ.

Points to Consider

- What is the main principle you've learned from this chapter? How will you apply it?
- Why do people have the tendency to follow formulas?
- Does your small group practice a balanced variety of activity? Why or why not?
- How has this chapter challenged you to press ahead and not give up?

APPENDIX A
WHAT DO YOU
NEED TO IMPROVE?

One of our principal goals in this book is to help churches find their weakest link and then work on that weak spot. Why? Because we know that thriving small groups are balanced and healthy in all areas—not just one or two. Just like we don't say a human body is healthy if all systems are working well except the heart, in the same way, church and small group health requires balance and needs all areas to be functioning normally.

Jim Egli has been developing a tool to find weak links for the last twenty years. At thrivingsmallgroups.com we've provided a way to determine the group's weakest obstacle which prevents a healthy, thriving group.

We've tested and retested the questions to provide the most

accurate results. We've reduced the survey questions to 35 from the original 110. After answering those questions, your group will discover their strengths and weaknesses. In this way, you can work on the weakest link, that area in your small group that prevents your group from thriving. Groups that thrive are healthy in each of the areas.

The good news is that it's free. This will make it easy for small groups to discover their weakest link, the area where they need to work the most.

APPENDIX B
RESEARCH DESIGN

I've used the plant analogy a lot to describe thriving groups, but a body analogy is similar. It's not enough to have a great heart if your lungs don't work or have kidneys that function well while your blood is prone to clotting. Good group health results from an overall normal experience. Our survey helps determine weaknesses in that experience.

Jim Egli wrote an excellent book, along with Dwight Marable, called *Small Groups, Big Impact*. The authors probed 3000 small group leaders about what does and does not make groups grow.

Egli's original research with Dwight Marable is solid, but it didn't go deep enough. We decided to ask additional questions about prayer, food, frequency and duration of meetings, and other elements. Granted the previous research gave us a strong data base, but it still needed refinement with response from deeper, more relevant questions.

Building on Egli's Original Study

In 2016, Jim Egli and Joel Comiskey added 1800 new surveys from leaders speaking English, Portuguese, Spanish, and Chinese. Adding different language groups broaden the research and helps us to generalize for a larger audience. We added this new research to Egli's previous investigation of over 3,000 small group leaders, so the correlations are quite significant. Again, our goal was to dive deeper into the small group itself--what does or does not make a healthy, thriving small group.

We aimed to discover what the leaders included in the meeting, what they did to prepare for the meeting, how well they cared for their members, and what the group did to reach out. We probed new areas like worship, Bible study material, icebreakers, ministry, prayer for unbelievers, and food. We wanted to know the critical factors that create thriving small groups.

We also asked questions about the leaders understanding of God's grace for themselves and others, and questions about sensitivity to the Holy Spirit. We wanted to know if these factors were more important than the behaviors themselves (Pray, Reach, Care, Empower).

How We Arrived At Our Findings

In previous studies, we tried to correlate leader behavior with growth, such as the leader's devotional life and evangelism with whether the group multiplied. Correlations are common in statistical studies and they are valid. But they can also be misleading. For example, for years, statisticians thought that coffee was bad for your health because correlations seemed to indicate this. What they didn't account for was that smokers drink more coffee than non-smokers. So the negative correlations between coffee and shortened life were not due to coffee itself but because of a strong relationship between smoking and coffee drinking. When coffee-drinking smokers were compared to non-coffee drinking smokers, and coffee-drinking nonsmokers were compared to non-coffee drinking nonsmokers, it became apparent that, rather than having a negative effective on longevity, drinking coffee has a slightly positive impact on how long people live.

Because correlations can be misleading, our research used two more advanced forms of statistical analysis: factor analysis and path analysis. Factor analysis uses multiple questions to measure each key group characteristic making measurements more accurate and reliable. Path analysis looks at multiple factors at once to discover which correlations are truly causal.

This data and analysis in this round of research again pointed to four pivotal small group factors that create thriving small groups. In previous books we labeled these four factors Upward, Inward, Outward, and Forward. Then more recently using action verbs: Pray, Care, Reach, and Empower. But this time we used a more advanced type of statistical analysis called MPlus which looks at the overall complex of factors and how they relate to one another. This revealed a larger overall factor encompassing those four factors, which we call simply Small Group Health.

Our analysis of small group data using multifactorial analysis revealed that prayer, care, outreach, and empowerment together created a larger factor best labeled simply "small group health" that is necessary for sustained small group growth.

To see the questions and take the survey, please see http://thrivingsmallgroups.com. For information about the exact questions we used or more details about the research design, please write: joelcomiskeyinfo@gmail.com.

Notes

1. 70-30 Principle: The small group leader talks only 30 percent of the time, while the members share 70 percent of the time. This should be the goal of every small group leader.
2. Roland Allen, *Missionary Methods: St. Paul's or Ours?* (Grand Rapids: Eerdmans, 1962), pp. 84-94.
3. Synonyms for Facilitate: Help, Aid, Assist, Ease, Make Easy, Empower, Lubricate, Smooth, Make Possible, Smooth the Progress
4. Inductive Bible study involves observation, interpretation, and application of a Bible verse or verses. It takes place when a person draws conclusions based on the plain biblical meaning, rather than simply accepting the commentary of an outside Bible authority.
5. Barbara J. Fleischer, *Facilitating for Growth* (Collegeville, MN: The Liturgical Press, 1993), p. 21.
6. Variety of Gifts Among Cell Leaders: When I polled 700 small leaders in eight countries, I discovered that no particular gift distinguished those who could multiply their group from those who could not. Here's how the leaders viewed their own giftedness:
   - Teaching   25.1%
   - Leadership   20.3%
   - Evangelism   19.0%
   - Pastoral care   10.6%
   - Mercy   10.6%
   - Other   14.4%

   No one particular gift stood out as more important. Small group leaders with the gift of teaching were no more prone to multiply their group than those with the gift of mercy. There was no one particular gift of the Spirit, such as evangelism, that distinguished those who could multiply their groups from those who could not.
7. Common Excuses for not Leading a Small Group

   Excuse #1: "I have very little time." All of us have the same amount of time to invest; the key question is how will you invest it.

   Excuse #2: "I haven't been trained." The basic prerequisites for leading an effective small group include: Love for Jesus, Love for his Word, and a desire to minister to others. Small group leaders never feel they have enough knowledge. All small group leaders are growing and learning.

Excuse #3: "I'm not mature enough in the Lord." If you're a young Christian, hungry for Jesus, with a desire to serve Him, leading a small group will provide an important stepping stone in your spiritual growth.

8. Joel Comiskey, *Home Cell Group Explosion* (Houston, TX: Touch Publications, 1998), p. 73.

9. Poll about Christian Influence The Institute for American Church Growth conducted a poll among 14,000 people from a variety of churches and denominations, asking them the question "Who or what was responsible for your coming to Christ and the church?" The results:
   - A special need—1-2%
   - Walk in—2-3%
   - Pastor—5-6%
   - Home visitation—1-2%
   - Sunday Schoo—4-5%
   - Evangelistic Crusade—0.5%
   - Church Program—2-3%
   - A Friend or Relative—75-90%

Wayne McDill's *Making Friends for Christ*, (Nashville, TN: Broadman Press, 1979, p. 28 & Jim Egli in Circle of Love.

10. Random Acts of Kindness: Alton P. LaBorde Sr. writes: "One of the key ways I've met and invited people to small groups is by helping people—strangers—who are in the process of moving. They may have a truck or a trailer loaded with furniture, and I just follow them to their destination and help them unload. On several occasions, I've used my truck and 16-foot-long trailer to assist them." (*Cell Church Magazine*, Summer 1999, p. 13).

11. Peggy Kannaday, ed. *Church Growth and the Home Cell System* (Seoul, Korea: Church Growth International, 1995), p. 19.

12 Dale Galloway, *20-20 Vision*, (Portland, OR: Scott Publishing, 1986) p. 144.

13 What is an *oikos*? The word *oikos* is found repeatedly in the New Testament, and is usually translated household. Today the word is used to refer to one's primary group of friends—those who relate directly to us through family, work, recreation, hobbies, and neighbors.

14. How to Pray for Non-Christians. Pray for God:
   - To give them a hunger for Christ.
   - To remove all barriers keeping them from responding to Christ.

- For God's blessing on each area of their lives.
- For the Holy Spirit to make Jesus real to them.

15. Praying for Non-Christians (Karen Hurston, "Preparing for Outreach through Evangelism-Based Prayer," Small Group Networks, July 2000)

- The "empty chair" prayer – Leave one chair empty during each group meeting to represent one or more lost friends. Ask your group members to gather around the chair and pray for the salvation of the lost people in their oikos (sphere of influence).
- Prayer partners – Pair up group members who will pray daily for each other's lost friends. These partners can hold each other accountable.
- Concert prayer for the lost – Introduce a new kind of prayer to your group! At your next meeting, ask them to stand and pray aloud simultaneously for the salvation of specific lost friends. It can be noisy, but it's a powerful "rumble" of prayer that puts Satan on notice!
- Prayer walking – Walk in pairs through a targeted community, praying for salvation to come to each home or apartment you walk past. This is a great way to prepare a new host home for your group meetings.
- Create a "Blessing List" or "Most Wanted" Poster – Use a pre-printed poster or a piece of butcher paper and write the names of lost people on it. Post it on the wall and pray for these people each week, making plans to connect them to the members between meetings.

16. Steps to Reach Out (I derived the basic steps from Janet Firebaugh's article, "Fishing Together," *Small Group Dynamics* (Small Group Network, October 1999).

- Each member targets one non-Christian contact (e.g., a family member, work associate, neighbor, etc.).
- Each group member commits himself (during the Works time) to initiate contact with that person within the next several weeks for the purpose of building their relationship. Invite these non-Christians into your life before inviting them to the group. Try to do things with them and serve them in the process.
- During each meeting (during the Works time), members share what happened with their contacts.
- The small group diligently prays for these people, as well as for the group member to continue to initiate contact. Pray that God will soften the hearts of the non-Christian friends. Ask Jesus to create opportunities for the building of friendships. Ask God to make it clear when the time is right to invite your friends to your group.

- A "harvest event" is scheduled for one month later. The idea is to plan a "neutral" group function—a dinner, a picnic, a women's luncheon, pizza party, video, etc. A one-day retreat or social functions that include a short devotional may be ways to ease your friends into the spiritual aspects of the group.
- Members begin inviting their contacts to the harvest event. Make your harvest event seeker-sensitive. Go to great lengths to make everyone feel welcome.
- Sell the importance of group life by talking about the benefits of the group. You can always talk about the many benefits of the group to your own life.
- Re-invite your friend to the group when the opportunity arises. Through ongoing prayer and follow-up, many invitees continue attending the small group and eventually the worship service.

17. Cho quoted in Karen Hurston, *Growing the World's Largest Church* (Springfield, MI: Chrism, 1994,) p. 107.

18 Creative Ideas for Inviting Non-Christians:
- Begin with a Barbecue. Many will come to a barbeque before attending a small group.
- Have the meeting at the home of the member who plans on inviting a new person. It's much easier for a non-Christian person to enter a "friend's home," rather than attend a meeting in a stranger's home.
- View parts of a secular video that lends itself to eternal questions.
- Plan a retreat with your group; go on a group bike ride; invite non-Christian friends to join the fun with you.
- Fill your empty chairs. Use some of the ideas above to invite new folks to your group.
- Look around on Sunday morning. Invite someone new or someone not in a group yet.

19. The Matthew Cell: The Matthew Cell is a break in the regular cell cycle wherein full attention is given to the people in our lives who need Christ, or need to follow him more seriously. Setting apart special time to focus on the people in our oikos (sphere of influence) is essential to help your group members persevere with unbelievers in their lives. One important note: through you may have special periodic meetings, such as the Matthew Cell, that focus on outreach, never forego the weekly "share the vision" time in your small group, where you articulate the goal of the group to multiply disciples. We must be encouraged regularly to press on with our relationships.

20. Mikel Neuman, *Home Groups for Urban Culture* (Pasadena, CA: William Carey Library, 1999) p. 82.

21. Used with permission from "Quest for the Perfect Pastoral System," p. 4. Pastor Harold F. Weitsz is the pastor of Little Fall Christian Centre, Little Falls, Roodepoort, South Africa. Presently, there are 2500 members and 200 cells.

22. Glen Martin & Gary McIntosh, *Creating Community* (Nashville, TN: Broadman & Holman Publishers, 1997), p. 113.

23. Howard A. Snyder, *The Radical Wesley* (Downers Grove, IL: Inter-Varsity Press, 1980), pp. 57,63 as quoted in Larry Kreider, *House to House* (Houston, TX: Touch Publications, 1995), p. 24.

24. Stephen Pile, *The Book of Failures*, quoted in Terry Powell, *You Can Lead a Bible Discussion Group!* (Sisters, OR: Mulnomah Books, 1996) p. 14.

25. Taken from the article by Greg Lee, "The Key to Growth: Multiplication," *Cell Church Magazine*, Winter, 1996: 15.

26. James M. Kouzes & Barry Z. Posner, p. 69.

27. Mark Glanville, "Jesus ate his way through the gospels – eaten with a tax-collector recently?" blogpost on July 20, 2012 at https://markrglanville. wordpress.com/2012/07/20/jesus-ate-his-way-through-the-gospels-eaten-with-a-tax-collector-recently/

28. Some would say that including a meal would be too much time and turn people off. However, our research uncovered that meeting length showed a positive correlation to people joining the group. Apparently, groups meeting longer experience more community that draws people in to the group. There was also a modest positive correlation with leadership multiplication and a mild negative correlation with the number of conversions. Apparently, groups meeting longer are experiencing more community which is drawing new people, and the longer meetings are giving more opportunity for leadership development, but people are slightly more hesitant to invite unbelievers to a longer meeting.

29. Almost twice as many group leaders in outreaching groups reported a strong level of intimacy (79%) as opposed to closed groups that didn't reach out (41%).

30. W.E. Vine and F.F. Bruce *Vine's Expository Dictionary of Old and New Testament Words*: W.E. Vine; Old Testament edited by F.F. Bruce (Old Tappan, N.J.: Revell, 1981). Vine defines the wordto signify the speaking forth of the mind and counsel of God: (pro, forth, phomi, to speak:

see prophet); in the New Testament it is used (a) of the gift, e.g., Romans 12:6; 1 Corinthians 12:10; 13:2; (b) either of the exercise of the gift or of that which is prophesied, e.g., Matthew 13:14; 1 Corinthians 13:8; 14:6, 22 and 1 Thessalonians 5:20, "prophesying (s);" 1 Timothy 1:18; 4:14; 2 Peter 1:20, 21; Revelation 1:3; 11:6; 19:10; 22:7, 10, 18, 19. Vine says, "Though much of O.T. prophecy was purely predictive, see Micah 5:2, e.g., and cp. John 11:51, prophecy is not necessarily, nor even primarily, fore-telling. It is the declaration of that which cannot be known by natural means, Matthew 26:68, it is the forth-telling of the will of God, whether with reference to the past, the present or the future, see Genesis 20:7; Deuteronomy 18:18; Revelation 10:11; 11:3."

31. Ralph Neighbour, audio tape. "From Structures to the Incarnation of Christ," 2003. Presented in Houston and accessed online at http://www.touchusa.org/avtraining.asp.

32. *Small Group Evangelism* (Pasadena, CA: Fuller Theological Seminary, 1996).

33. Peace, p. 27.

34. "The Door" by Sam Shoemaker

I admire the people who go way in.

But I wish they would not forget how it was

Before they got in. Then they would be able to help

The people who have not yet even found the door;

Or the people who want to run away again from God.

You can go in too deeply, and stay in too long,

And forget the people outside the door.

As for me, I shall take my accustomed place,

Near enough to God to hear Him, and know He is there,

But not so far from men as not to hear them,

And remember they are there, too.

Where? Outside the door -

Thousands of them, millions of them.

But - more important for me -

One of them, two of them, ten of them.

Whose hands I am intended to put on the latch.

So I shall stay by the door and wait

For those who seek it.

"I had rather be a door-keeper..."

So I stay near the door.

35. "10 Reasons Not to Reach Out" (Jimmy Long, Anny Beyerlein, Sara Keiper, Patty Pell, Nina Thiel and Doug Whalon, *Small Groups Leader's Handbook*, Downer's Grove, IL: InterVarsity Press, 1995, p. 87)
   • If people start becoming Christians, we'll need a bigger room to meet in.
   • Praying for two friends to come to know Jesus isn't in my job description.
   • If everyone in my small group wants to go to India this summer, I'll have to go too.
   • Taking risks isn't good for my disposition.
   • If we become known as Christians in our dorm, people might start asking us questions about our faith.
   • Revival isn't in my one-year plan.
   • Serving the poor might make me uncomfortable with my lifestyle.
   • If our group stays small, everything will be under control.
   • Telling people about Jesus isn't politically correct.
   • Trusting God to use our small group to make a difference on campus, in the community and in the world is too much to ask.

36. Howard A.Snyder, *The Radical Wesley & Patterns for Church Renewal* (Downers Grove, IL: Inter-Varsity Press, 1980), p. 55.

37. Eddie Gibbs, *Church Next* (Downer's Grove, IL: InterVarsity Press, 2000), p. 183.

38. Larry Crabb, *Connecting* (Nashville: Word Publishing, 1997), p. 31.

39. This is not to ignore the vital role that experienced and profession care-givers, therapists, and psychologists play in the healing of hurt and damaged people. Some traumas that people experience require expert help.

40. David Lowes Watson, *The Early Methodist Class Meeting* (Nashville, TN: Discipleship Resources, 1987), pp. 193-195.

41. Ibid., Kindle Locations 802-808.

42. Touch Publications sells a book dedicated entirely to icebreakers (call 1-800-735-5865 or go to www.touchusa.org) NavPress sells an excellent book called *101 Best Small Group Ideas* (Colorado Springs, CO: NavPress Publishing Group, 1996; http://www.navpress.com/. The *Serendipity Bible* is loaded with excellent icebreaker questions: http://www.serendipityhouse.com/pages/home.html

43. Stephen J. Dubner and Steven D. Levitt, "A Star is Born," *New York Times* magazine (May 07, 2006). Accessed at: http://www.nytimes.com/2006/05/07/magazine/07wwln_freak.html

44. Jim Collins, *Good to Great* (New York, NY: HarperCollins Publishers, Inc.

2001), p. 14.

45. Colin Powell leadership quotes at http://www.leadershipgeeks.com/col-in-powell-leadership/. Accessed on Saturday, December 30, 2017.

RESOURCES

BY

JOEL COMISKEY

You can find all of Joel Comiskey's books at:
www.joelcomiskeygroup.com
Phone: 1-888-511-9995
email: joelcomiskeyinfo@gmail.com

Joel Comiskey's previous books cover the following topics

- Leading a cell group (*How to Lead a Great Cell Group Meeting*, 2001, 2009; *Children in Cell Ministry*, 2016; *Youth in Cell Ministry*, 2016).

- How to multiply the cell group (*Home Cell Group Explosion*, 1998).

- How to prepare spiritually for cell ministry (*An Appointment with the King*, 2002, 2011).

- How to practically organize your cell system (*Reap the Harvest*, 1999; *Cell Church Explosion*, 2004).

- How to train future cell leaders (*Leadership Explosion*, 2001; *Live*, 2007; *Encounter*, 2007; *Grow*, 2007; *Share*, 2007; *Lead*, 2007; *Coach*, 2008; *Discover*, 2008).

- How to coach/care for cell leaders (*How to be a Great Cell Group Coach*, 2003; *Groups of Twelve*, 2000; *From Twelve to Three*, 2002).

- How the gifts of the Spirit work within the cell group (*The Spirit-filled Small Group*, 2005, 2009; *Discover*, 2008).

- How to fine tune your cell system (*Making Cell Groups Work Navigation Guide*, 2003).

- Principles from the second largest church in the world (*Passion and Persistence*, 2004).

- How cell church works in North America (*The Church that Multiplies*, 2007, 2009).

- How to plant a church (*Planting Churches that Reproduce*, 2009)

- How to be a relational disciple (*Relational Disciple*, 2010).

- How to distinguish truth from myths *(Myths and Truths of the Cell Church*, 2011).

- What the Biblical foundations for cell church are *(Biblical Foundations for the Cell-Based Church*, 2012, *Making Disciples in the Cell-Based Church*, 2013, *2000 Years of Small Groups, 2015*).

All of the books listed are available from Joel Comiskey Group
www.joelcomiskeygroup.com

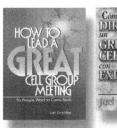

How To Lead A Great Cell Group Meeting:
So People Want to Come Back

Do people expectantly return to your group meetings every week? Do you have fun and experience joy during your meetings? Is everyone participating in discussion and ministry? You can lead a great cell group meeting, one that is life changing and dynamic. Most people don't realize that they can create a God-filled atmosphere because they don't know how. Now the secret is out. This guide will show you how to:

- Prepare yourself spiritually to hear God during the meeting
- Structure the meeting so it flows
- Spur people in the group to participate and share their lives openly
- Share your life with others in the group
- Create stimulating questions
- Listen effectively to discover what is transpiring in others' lives
- Encourage and edify group members
- Open the group to non-Christians
- See the details that create a warm atmosphere

By implementing these time-tested ideas, your group meetings will become the hot-item of your members' week. They will go home wanting more and return each week bringing new people with them. 140 pgs.

Home Cell Group Explosion: *How Your Small Group Can Grow and Multiply*

The book crystallizes the author's findings in some eighteen areas of research, based on a meticulous questionnaire that he submitted to cell church leaders in eight countries around the world, locations that he also visited personally for his research. The detailed notes in the back of the book offer the student of cell church growth a rich mine for further reading. The beauty of Comiskey's book is that he not only summarizes his survey results in a thoroughly convincing way but goes on to analyze in practical ways many of his survey results in separate chapters. The happy result is that any cell church leader, intern or member completing this quick read will have his priorities/values clearly aligned and ready to be followed-up. If you are a pastor or small group leader, you should devour this book! It will encourage you and give you simple, practical steps for dynamic small group life and growth. 175 pgs.

An Appointment with the King: *Ideas for Jump-Starting Your Devotional Life*

With full calendars and long lists of things to do, people often put on hold life's most important goal: building an intimate relationship with God. Often, believers wish to pursue the goal but are not sure how to do it. They feel frustrated or guilty when their attempts at personal devotions seem empty and unfruitful. With warm, encouraging writing, Joel Comiskey guides readers on how to set a daily appointment with the King and make it an exciting time they will look forward to. This book first answers the question "Where do I start?" with step-by-step instructions on how to spend time with God and practical ideas for experiencing him more fully. Second, it highlights the benefits of spending time with God, including joy, victory over sin, and spiritual guidance. The book will help Christians tap into God's resources on a daily basis, so that even in the midst of busyness they can walk with him in intimacy and abundance. 175 pgs.

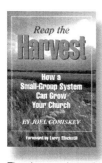

Reap the Harvest: *How a Small Group System Can Grow System Can Grow Your Church*

Have you tried small groups and hit a brick wall? Have you wondered why your groups are not producing the fruit that was promised? Are you looking to make your small groups more effective? Cell-church specialist and pastor Dr. Joel Comiskey studied the world's most successful cell churches to determine why they grow. The key: They have embraced specific principles. Conversely, churches that do not embrace these same principles have problems with their groups and therefore do not grow. Cell churches are successful not because they have small groups but because they can support the groups. In this book, you will discover how these systems work. 236 pgs.

La Explosión de la Iglesia Celular: *Cómo Estructurar la Iglesia en Células Eficaces* (Editorial Clie, 2004)

This book is available only in Spanish and contains Joel Comiskey's research of eight of the world's largest cell churches, five of which reside in Latin America. It details how to make the transition from a traditional church to the cell church structure and many other valuable insights, including: the history of the cell church, how to organize your church to become a praying church, the most important principles of the cell church, and how to raise up an army of cell leaders. 236 pgs.

182

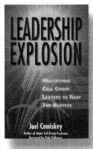

Leadership Explosion: *Multiplying Cell Group Leaders to Reap the Harvest*

Some have said that cell groups are leader breeders. Yet even the best cell groups often have a leadership shortage. This shortage impedes growth and much of the harvest goes untouched. Joel Comiskey has discovered why some churches are better at raising up new cell leaders than others. These churches do more than pray and hope for new leaders. They have an intentional strategy, a plan that will quickly equip as many new leaders as possible. In this book, you will discover the training models these churches use to multiply leaders. You will discover the underlying principles of these models so that you can apply them. 202 pgs.

FIVE-BOOK EQUIPPING SERIES

#1: Live   #2: Encounter   #3: Grow   #4: Share   #5: Lead

The five book equipping series is designed to train a new believer all the way to leading his or her own cell group. Each of the five books contains eight lessons. Each lesson has interactive activities that helps the trainee reflect on the lesson in a personal, practical way.

Live starts the training by covering key Christian doctrines, including baptism and the Lord's supper. 85 pgs.

Encounter guides the believer to receive freedom from sinful bondages. The Encounter book can be used one-on-one or in a group. 91 pgs.

Grow gives step-by-step instruction for having a daily quiet time, so that the believer will be able to feed him or herself through spending daily time with God. 87 pgs.

Share instructs the believer how to communicate the gospel message in a winsome, personal way. This book also has two chapters on small group evangelism. 91 pgs.

Lead prepares the Christian on how to facilitate an effective cell group. This book would be great for those who form part of a small group team. 91 pgs.

TWO-BOOK ADVANCED TRAINING SERIES

Coach   Discover

Coach and *Discover* make-up the Advanced Training, prepared specifically to take a believer to the next level of maturity in Christ.

Coach prepares a believer to coach another cell leader. Those experienced in cell ministry often lack understanding on how to coach someone else. This book provides step-by-step instruction on how to coach a new cell leader from the first meeting all the way to giving birth to a new group. The book is divided into eight lessons, which are interactive and help the potential coach deal with real-life, practical coaching issues. 85 pgs.

Discover clarifies the twenty gifts of the Spirit mentioned in the New Testament. The second part shows the believer how to find and use his or her particular gift. This book is excellent to equip cell leaders to discover the giftedness of each member in the group. 91 pgs.

How to be a Great Cell Group Coach: Practical insight for Supporting and Mentoring Cell Group Leaders

Research has proven that the greatest contributor to cell group success is the quality of coaching provided for cell group leaders. Many are serving in the position of a coach, but they don't fully understand what they are supposed to do in this position. Joel Comiskey has identified seven habits of great cell group coaches. These include: Receiving from God, Listening to the needs of the cell group leader, Encouraging the cell group leader, Caring for the multiple aspects of a leader's life, Developing the cell leader in various aspects of leadership, Strategizing with the cell leader to create a plan, Challenging the cell leader to grow.

Practical insights on how to develop these seven habits are outlined in section one. Section two addresses how to polish your skills as a coach with instructions on diagnosing problems in a cell group, how to lead coaching meetings, and what to do when visiting a cell group meeting. This book will prepare you to be a great cell group coach, one who mentors, supports, and guides cell group leaders into great ministry. 139 pgs.

Groups of Twelve: *A New Way to Mobilize Leaders and Multiply Groups in Your Church*

This book clears the confusion about the Groups of 12 model. Joel dug deeply into the International Charismatic Mission in Bogota, Colombia and other G12 churches to learn the simple principles that G12 has to offer your church. This book also contrasts the G12 model with the classic 5x5 and shows you what to do with this new model of ministry. Through onsite research, international case studies, and practical experience, Joel Comiskey outlines the G12 principles that your church can use today.

Billy Hornsby, director of the Association of Related Churches, says, "Joel Comiskey shares insights as a leader who has himself raised up numerous leaders. From how to recognize potential leaders to cell leader training to time-tested principles of leadership—this book has it all. The accurate comparisons of various training models make it a great resource for those who desire more leaders. Great book!" 182 pgs.

From Twelve To Three: *How to Apply G12 Principles in Your Church*

The concept of the Groups of 12 began in Bogota, Colombia, but now it is sweeping the globe. Joel Comiskey has spent years researching the G12 structure and the principles behind it.

From his experience as a pastor, trainer, and consultant, he has discovered that there are two ways to embrace the G12 concept: adopting the entire model or applying the principles that support the model.

This book focuses on the application of principles rather than adoption of the entire model. It outlines the principles and provides a modified application which Joel calls the G12.3. This approach presents a pattern that is adaptable to many different church contexts.

The concluding section illustrates how to implement the G12.3 in various kinds of churches, including church plants, small churches, large churches, and churches that already have cells. 178 pgs.

The Spirit-filled Small Group: *Leading Your Group to Experience the Spiritual Gifts.*

The focus in many of today's small groups has shifted from Spirit-led transformation to just another teacher-student Bible study. But exercising every member's spiritual gifts is vital to the effectiveness of the group. With insight born of experience in more than twenty years of small group ministry, Joel Comiskey explains how leaders and participants alike can be supernaturally equipped to deal with real-life issues. Put these principles into practice and your small group will never be the same!

This book works well with Comiskey's training book, **Discover.** It fleshes out many of the principles in Comiskey's training book. Chuck Crismier, radio host, *Viewpoint,* writes, "Joel Comiskey has again provided the Body of Christ with an important tool to see God's Kingdom revealed in and through small groups." 191 pgs.

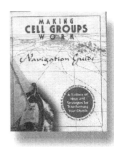

Making Cell Groups Work Navigation Guide: *A Toolbox of Ideas and Strategies for Transforming Your Church.*

For the first time, experts in cell group ministry have come together to provide you with a page reference tool like no other. When Ralph Neighbour, Bill Beckham, Joel Comiskey and Randall Neighbour compiled new articles and information under careful orchestration and in-depth understanding that Scott Boren brings to the table, it's as powerful as private consulting! Joel Comiskey has an entire book within this mammoth page work. There are also four additional authors.

Passion and Persistence: *How the Elim Church's Cell Groups Penetrated an Entire City for Jesus*

This book describes how the Elim Church in San Salvador grew from a small group to 116,000 people in 10,000 cell groups. Comiskey takes the principles from Elim and applies them to churches in North America and all over the world. Ralph Neighbour says: "I believe this book will be remember as one of the most important ever written about a cell church movement! I experienced the passion when visiting Elim many years ago. Comiskey's report about Elim is not a pattern to be slavishly copied. It is a journey into grasping the true theology and methodology of the New Testament church. You'll discover how the Elim Church fans into flame their passion for Jesus and His Word, how they organize their cells to penetrate a city and world for Jesus, and how they persist until God brings the fruit." 158 pgs.

The Church that Multiplies: *Growing a Healthy Cell Church in North America*

Does the cell church strategy work in North America? We hear about exciting cell churches in Colombia and Korea, but where are the dynamic North American cell churches? This book not only declares that the cell church concept does work in North America but dedicates an entire chapter to examining North American churches that are successfully using the cell strategy to grow in quality and quantity. This book provides the latest statistical research about the North American church and explains why the cell church approach restores health and growth to the church today. More than anything else, this book will provide practical solutions for pastors and lay leaders to use in implementing cell-based ministry. 181 pgs.

Planting Churches that Reproduce: *Planting a Network of Simple Churches*

What is the best way to plant churches in the 21st century? Comiskey believes that simple, reproducible church planting is most effective. The key is to plant churches that are simple enough to grow into a movement of churches. Comiskey has been gathering material for this book for the past fifteen Years. He has also planted three churches in a wide variety of settings. Planting Churches that Reproduce is the fruit of his research and personal experience. Comiskey uses the latest North American church planting statistics, but extends the illustrations to include worldwide church planting. More than anything else, this book will provide practical solutions for those planting churches today. Comiskey's book is a must-read book for all those interested in establishing Christ-honoring, multiplying churches. 176 pgs.

The Relational Disciple: *How God Uses Community to Shape Followers of Jesus*

Jesus lived with His disciples for three years and taught them life lessons as a group. After three years, he commanded them to "go and do likewise" (Matthew 28:18-20). Jesus discipled His followers through relationships—and He wants us to do the same. Scripture is full of exhortations to love and serve one another. This book will show you how. The isolation present in the western world is creating a hunger for community and the world is longing to see relational disciples in action. This book will encourage Christ-followers to allow God to use the natural relationships in life—family, friends, work relationships, cells, church, and missions to mold them into relational disciples.

187

You Can Coach: *How to Help Leaders Build Healthy Churches through Coaching*

We've entitled this book "You Can Coach" because we believe that coaching is more about passing on what you've lived and holding others accountable in the process. Coaching doesn't require a higher degree, special talent, unique personality, or a particular spiritual gift. We believe, in fact, that God wants coaching to become a movement. We long to see the day in which every pastor has a coach and in turn is coaching someone else. In this book, you'll hear three coaches who have successfully coached pastors for many years. They will share their history, dreams, principles, and what God is doing through coaching. Our hope is that you'll be both inspired and resourced to continue your own coaching ministry in the years to come.

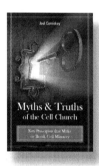

Myths & Truths of the Cell Church: *Key Principles that Make or Break Cell Ministry*

Most of the modern day cell church movement is dynamic, positive, and applicable. As is true in most endeavors, errors and false assumptions have also cropped up to destroy an otherwise healthy movement. Sometimes these false concepts caused the church to go astray completely. At other times, they led the pastor and church down a dead-end road of fruitless ministry. Regardless of how the myths were generated, they had a chilling effect on the church's ministry. In this book, Joel Comiskey tackles these errors and false assumptions, helping pastors and leaders to untangle the webs of legalism that has crept into the cell church movement. Joel then guides the readers to apply biblical, time-tested principles that will guide them into fruitful cell ministry. Each chapter begins with a unique twist. Well-known worldwide cell church leaders open each chapter by answering questions to the chapter's topic in the form of an email dialogue. Whether you're starting out for the first time in cell ministry or a seasoned veteran, this book will give you the tools to help your ministry stay fresh and fruitful.

Biblical Foundations for the Cell-Based Church

Why cell church? Is it because David Cho's church is a cell church and happens to be the largest church in the history of Christianity? Is it because cell church is the strategy that many "great" churches are using?

Ralph Neighbour repeatedly says, "Theology must breed methodology."Joel Comiskey has arrived at the same conclusion. Biblical truth is the only firm foundation for anything we do. Without a biblical base, we don't have a strong under-pinning upon which we can hang our ministry and philosophy. We can plod through most anything when we know that God is stirring us to behave biblically.

Making Disciples in the Cell-Based Church

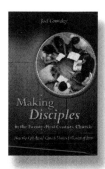

The primary goal of the church is to make disciples who make disciples. But how is the church supposed to do that? This book answers that question. Dr. Comiskey explains how both cell and celebration (larger gathering) work together in the process of making disciples. In the cell, a potential disciple is transformed through community, priesthood of all believers, group evangelism, and team multiplication. The cell system ensures each leader has a coach and that training happens. Then the cells gather together to worship and grow through the teaching of God's Word. This book will help you understand why and how to become a church that prioritizes discipleship.

What others are saying: I've read all of Joel Comiskey's books, but this one is his best work yet. I'm looking forward to having all of our pastors, coaches, cell leaders and members read this book in the near future. *Dr. Dennis Watson, Lead Pastor, Celebration Church of New Orleans*

I am so excited about Joel Comiskey's new book, Making Disciples in the Twenty-First Century Church. Joel has unpacked discipleship, not just as an endeavor for individuals, but as the critical element for creating a church community and culture that reproduces the Kingdom of God all over the earth. *Jimmy Seibert, Senior Pastor, Antioch Community Church*

Like Joel's other books, this one is solidly biblical, highly practical, wonderfully accessible and is grounded in Joel's vast research and experience. *Dr. Dave Earley, Lead Pastor, Grace City Church of Las Vegas, Nevada*

189

2000 Years of Small Groups: A History of Cell Ministry in the Church

This book explores how God has used small groups throughout church history, specifically focusing on the early church to the present time. God not only established the early church as a house to house movement, but he also has used small groups throughout church history. This book chronicles the small group or cell movement from Jesus all the way to the modern day cell explosion. Themes include:Small Groups In Biblical History, Small Groups In Early Christian History, Small Groups and Monasticism, Small Groups During the Pre-Reformation Period, Luther and Small Groups, Martin Bucer and Small Groups, The Anabaptist Movement, Puritan Conventicles, Pietism, The Moravians, The Methodists, Modern House Churches, Small Groups in North America, and The Modern Day Cell Church. This book will both critique the strengths and weaknesses of these historical movements and apply principles to today's church.

Children in Cell Ministry: Discipling the Future Generation Now

Joel Comiskey challenges pastors and leaders to move from simply educating children to forming them into disciples who make disciples. Comiskey lays out the Biblical base for children's ministry and then encourages pastors and leaders to formulate their own vision and philosophy for ministry to children based on the Biblical text. Comiskey highlights how to disciple children in both the large group and the small group. He quickly moves into practical examples of intergenerational cell groups and how effective cell churches have implemented this type of group. He then writes about children only cell groups, citing many practical examples from some of the most effective cell churches in the world. Comiskey covers equipping for children, how to equip the parents, and mistakes in working with children in the cell church. This book will help those wanting to minister to children both in large and small groups.

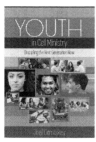

Youth in Cell Ministry: Discipling the Future Generation

If we are going to have a victorious church tomorrow, we must focus on the youth today. In this book, Comiskey lays out the biblical base for youth ministry, highlights the felt needs of today's youth, and then shows why small groups are the most effective way to make youth disciples today. Comiskey explains the difference between inter-generational cells and student-led groups, the equipping process for youth leaders, how to coach leaders, and how to get started in youth cell ministry. Comiskey also describes common errors in youth ministry and how to avoid them. This book is a must-read for all those wanting to make youth disciples through cell ministry..

Humility is key be no matter how badly I may want a group to grow toward God, I will never be able to do that on my own merit

A good group doesn't depend on the leader's strength, but the leaders reliance on God and others to support his weaknesses

While a group's outreach can go beyond the leaders influence, the group can be limited by the lack of investment the leader puts into it.

Made in the USA
Middletown, DE
02 May 2018